GRANT WOOD AND
Little Sister Nan
• ESSAYS AND REMEMBRANCES •

Nan Wood Graham's favorite photograph of herself with a print of the painting American Gothic. *Right: A portrait of the artist Grant Wood, brother of Nan Wood Graham and the creator of* American Gothic.

by
Julie Jensen McDonald
with
Joan Liffring-Zug Bourret
contributing editor

Penfield
Press

Acknowledgements

In addition to those listed with their essays in this book, we wish to thank: Steven Bradley, director, Davenport Museum of Art; Leslie Wright, former curator, Lou Wendel and Mary Westphalen, Cedar Rapids Museum of Art; Pam White Trimpe, curator of paintings, The University of Iowa Museum of Art; Helen Glasson, Eldon, Iowa; John Johnson, Iowa City; Maria Miltner Stender, Indiatlantic, Florida; Phyllis Fleming, *Cedar Rapids Gazette* editor; William Bilsland III and Curt and Norma Hames, Cedar Rapids; Laurence F. Jonson, AACR, Deere Art Collection Curator, Moline, Illinois; Robert Panzer, director VAGA, New York, N.Y., and Peggy Cleeton and the Julin Printing Company, Monticello, Iowa.

"Grant Wood remembered" and other excerpts are from scrapbooks started by Nan Wood Graham in the 1930s. Nan donated this collection to the Davenport Museum of Art in 1986. Additional text is from the book *This Is Grant Wood Country*, 1978, (now out of print). Grant Wood drawings, courtesy the Cedar Rapids Community School District.

Photographs are from the collections of Joan Liffring-Zug Bourret, the State Historical Society of Iowa, the Cedar Rapids Museum of Art, Davenport Museum of Art, and John Fitzpatrick. Title page photograph: Grant Wood, by Kadgihn, Iowa City. The photographer of Nan's favorite pose of herself is unknown.

Prologue, page 6, and Epilogue, page 136, illustrations are by Grant Wood, from the 1908 yearbook.

Front cover: Nan Wood Graham and Dr. Byron McKeeby, models for *American Gothic*, posed together for the first time with the painting, loaned by the Art Institute of Chicago, at the 1942 Grant Wood Memorial Exhibition of 70 paintings, Cedar Rapids Public Library Gallery. Photograph by John Reynolds, *Cedar Rapids Gazette*.

Back cover: Beam's Choice Decanter, Gothic Parody Collection, Davenport Museum of Art.

Associate editors: Dorothy Crum, Melinda Bradnan, Greta Anderson. Graphics editor: Molly Cook, M.A. Cook Design, Cedar Rapids.

Books by Mail (postpaid):
Grant Wood and Little Sister Nan (this book) $20.95
My Brother, Grant Wood by Nan Wood Graham $20.95
The American Gothic Cookbook (recipes by Grant, Nan and others) $8.95
To order write: Penfield Press • 215 Brown Street • Iowa City, Iowa 52245

Foreword

Nan Wood Graham may be one of the most widely recognized images in the entire world. As the woman immortalized in Grant Wood's famous painting, *American Gothic*, she symbolically represents midwestern women and the roles they have played. Far more important than this single iconographic image is the life that Nan Wood Graham led as an artist in her own right. Although known for celebrating and promoting the life and work of her brother Grant Wood, she merits acclaim for her own creative impulses, both as a painter and biographer.

The State Historical Society of Iowa is privileged to have a rare painting by Nan Wood Graham entitled *Boarding House Bathroom*. Colorful and humorous, her artistic rendering of a crudely furnished and ill-kept bathroom immediately brings a laugh to the viewer. In an almost cartoonish fashion, she championed kitsch in the art world by choosing such unusual and somewhat taboo subjects as a toilet and stained linoleum. Portraying a figure that resembles Grant Wood in a bathrobe, she pokes fun at a situation she was familiar with if not altogether happy with. She even uses a metallic, reflective paint for the mirror surface. The painting serves as evidence of her artistic flair for life and her talent for portraying the ordinary in a humorous fashion.

The State Historical Society of Iowa also had the pleasure of publishing her book, *My Brother, Grant Wood*, a landmark study of Iowa's most famous painter. She shares stories that only she as a sister could know. Her own story is inextricably woven into the story of her brother, and we are indeed fortunate that she preserved her memories in a permanent form that can be shared with others.

Grant Wood and Little Sister Nan: Essays and Remembrances draws Nan Wood Graham out of the larger tapestry of Wood's life and gives definition to her loyal support of her brother and her own achievements. She was a pathfinder whose contributions extend into areas that cannot be easily measured.

—Mary Bennett, Special Collections Coordinator
State Historical Society of Iowa

Dedicated to
Nan (Nicky) Wood Graham

"...fierce guardian of the truths of her brother's life, who let no myth or falsehood go unchallenged. Discharging this responsibility involved no hostility on her part, however. She knew which writer originated each inaccuracy, and she wanted the record set straight, but she did not want their names used. She thought they all deserved obscurity."

—Julie Jensen McDonald

Joan Liffring-Zug Bourret photograph, 1975

Nan Wood Graham in the living room of her Riverside, California ranch home. She is holding a jug decorated with a depiction of American Gothic. *On the wall are Grant Wood lithographs, hand-colored by Nan and her husband Edward. Following Wood's master set, they painted 996 of the* Wild Flowers, Tame Flowers, Fruits, *and* Vegetables *lithographs. Originally sold for $10 each, they now bring thousands of dollars each.*

Contents

Prologue

Nameless Faces—World Famous Models

As symbols of humor and satire recreated in thousands of publications, Nan Wood Graham and Dr. Byron McKeeby, models for Grant Wood's *American Gothic* painting, are unsurpassed. Nan and Dr. McKeeby, formerly of Cedar Rapids, Iowa, have been parodied individually and together since the late 1930s. They are symbolic portraits recognized as uniquely American.

Childless, Nan Wood Graham enthusiastically dedicated herself, from middle-age until her death, to protect her brother Grant's memory, reflecting her belief in his greatness. We who knew Nan loved her for her graciousness and charm.

Grant Wood's legacy to the art world is apparent. His bequest to Nan Wood Graham was at least twofold: with *American Gothic* he assured her a unique place in the history of American painting and, on a more personal level, he left her the many warm memories of being sister to one of this country's foremost artists.

—Joan Liffring-Zug Bourret, publisher, Penfield Press

1979 Parody of Nan holding the Daughters of Revolution *tea cup by Esther Feske*

Joan Liffring-Zug Bourret 1975 photo

Nan Wood Graham stands in her living room between prints of her brother's masterpieces, American Gothic *and* Woman With Plant(s).

Passages in Time

1891 Grant DeVolson Wood was born February 13, on a farm near Anamosa, Iowa, the second child of Quaker parents Francis M. and Hattie D. Weaver Wood.

1899 Nancy Rebecca Wood was born in the farmhouse near Anamosa, Iowa, on July 19, the fourth child of the Woods.

1901 Francis Maryville Wood died on March 17. In September, Mrs. Wood, her three sons, Frank, John, and Grant, and baby daughter Nan moved to Cedar Rapids.

1905 Grant Wood's colored drawing of an oak leaf won a national Crayola contest prize.

1910–1911 Grant Wood, nicknamed "Gussie," graduated from Washington High School in Cedar Rapids and attended summer school two summers at the Minneapolis School of Design and Handicraft and Normal Art.

1911–1912 Grant Wood taught at Rosedale country school, Cedar Rapids, and attended night classes in life drawing at the University of Iowa.

1913–1916 These years Wood spent in Cedar Rapids and in Chicago. He attended night classes at the Art Institute of Chicago and worked days as a designer at Kalo Silversmith Shop. Nan lived with her brother, Frank Wood, and attended high school in Waterloo, Iowa.

1917 Hattie Wood lost the family home in Cedar Rapids through foreclosure, and Grant built a house in the Kenwood Heights area for his mother and Nan. Grant gave Nan his painting, *Quivering Aspen*, for her eighteenth birthday.

1918 As a World War I soldier, Grant designed artillery camouflage in Washington, D.C. He also drew sketches of fellow doughboys. Nan graduated from Kenwood Park High School, May 21.

1919 Grant Wood began teaching at Jackson Junior High School, Cedar Rapids. In his first exhibition, he showed 23 small paintings in a two-man show with artist Marvin Cone at Killian's department store in Cedar Rapids. Nan graduated from Cedar Rapids Business College.

1920 Grant Wood and Marvin Cone spent the summer in Paris, painting. This was the first of Wood's four trips to Europe. He continued teaching at Jackson School. Nan worked for Emma Grattan, supervisor of art in the Cedar Rapids schools.

1922 Grant Wood became art teacher at McKinley High School, Cedar Rapids.

1923 Grant studied at the Academie Julien in Paris. He also painted in Italy and in the French provinces. Nan toured Canada and Alaska with Aunt Sarah (Sallie) and Uncle Clarence Wood.

1924 Wood remodeled the carriage house loft at #5 Turner Alley, as a home for Nan and his mother and a studio for himself. Nan married Emmett Edward Graham August 1, at the courthouse in Marion, Iowa. A newspaper account read, "The marriage came as a surprise to friends of the couple."

1925 Wood was commissioned to do paintings of workers at Cherry Company, a dairy equipment manufacturing plant. Nan's husband Ed Graham entered Oakdale Sanitarium, Iowa City, for treatment of tuberculosis.

1926 Grant Wood made his third trip to Europe. He exhibited 47 paintings at Galerie Carmine, Paris, sold a few, and brought others home.

1927 Wood was commissioned to design and build a large stained-glass window for the Veterans' Memorial Coliseum in Cedar Rapids. Nan posed as the woman representing the Republic in the window. Wood retired from public school teaching. Nan traveled to Texas with Clarence and Sallie Wood. Aunt Sallie died on the trip.

1928 Wood went to Munich, Germany to supervise work on the stained-glass and the window, and painted some of the glass himself. On this trip, he became interested in Flemish and German painting.

1929 Grant Wood painted *John B. Turner, Pioneer*, and *Woman with Plant(s)* in his new style. Nan entered Oakdale Sanitarium for treatment of tuberculosis, weighing only ninety-seven pounds. Regaining her health, she put on thirty-one pounds.

Photographs of Youthful Grant and Nan

Grant Wood, age 10, the year his father died and the year of his first recognized drawing, a hen sitting on eggs. 1901

Nancy Rebecca Wood, age 4, named after her grandmother Rebecca Wood. 1903

Above: Nan, age 22. 1921 Left: Nan, age 18, by the Kenwood home, Cedar Rapids, Iowa. 1917

Wood Family Homes

Above: Four children, John, Frank, Grant, and Nan were born in this Wood family farmhouse, four miles east of Anamosa, Iowa. The house was destroyed by fire in 1974.

Right: The "shack" Grant built in Cedar Rapids after his mother lost their home to foreclosure in 1917. Grant, Nan and their mother spent a summer there. Later, Grant built the home shown below at 3178 Grove Court SE, where they lived until 1924.

1930 Nan lived with her mother and Grant at #5 Turner Alley and posed for *American Gothic*. *American Gothic* was entered in the Annual Exhibition of American Paintings and Sculpture at the Art Institute of Chicago and won the Norman Wait Harris Bronze Medal and the $300 Purchase Award. It was an instant sensation and has remained the property of the Art Institute of Chicago ever since. *Stone City* won the landscape prize of the Art Salon at the Iowa State Fair.

1931–1932 During these productive years, Grant Wood painted *Midnight Ride of Paul Revere, The Appraisal, Victorian Survival, Birthplace of Herbert Hoover, Young Corn, Fall Plowing, Daughters of Revolution, Arbor Day, Fruits of Iowa, Autumn Oaks, Self-Portrait*, and others. He founded and taught at the Stone City Colony and Art School for two summers. Nan won first prize in an art show for a hand-tooled leather purse. Nan's face was burned as she helped her mother down the stairs during a January 14 fire in a storeroom at #5 Turner Alley. Nan and Ed moved to Albuquerque.

1933–1934 Grant Wood was named Iowa director of the Federal Public Works of Art Project (PWAP) and supervised the painting of murals for the Iowa State University Library. He completed *Dinner for Threshers* and joined the faculty at the University of Iowa, Iowa City, as an Associate Professor of Fine Arts. Nan sat for her portrait in 1933, the last time she would pose for her brother.

1935 Grant Wood married Sara S. Maxon and honeymooned at the Heights Hotel, McGregor, Iowa. They moved into and restored a Civil War era home in Iowa City. One-man exhibitions of Wood's work were held at the Ferargil Galleries, New York, and at Lakeside Press Galleries, Chicago. Wood was elected to the National Society of Mural Painters. He painted *Death on the Ridge Road*. He began lecture tours which continued each year until his death. Grant asked Nan to come home because their mother was ill. Hattie Weaver Wood died October 11.

1936 Along with his teaching and lecturing, Wood painted *Spring Turning*.

1937 Wood did many of his black-and-white lithographs, and began the set of four tinted lithographs as black-and-white prints which Nan Wood Graham and her husband Edward colored. He completed illustrations for a Limited Editions edition of Sinclair Lewis's *Main Street*.

1938 Nan exhibited her reverse glass paintings in New York. The Grahams drove Sara Maxon Wood, Grant's estranged wife, to California. Nan and Ed would live there for the rest of their lives.

1939 Grant and Sara were divorced. Grant painted *Parson Weems' Fable*, and taught Nan how to tint his lithographs; she taught Ed, and they earned much-needed money.

1940–1941 On sabbatical leave from the University, Wood continued to lecture. He did a *Time* magazine cover of Henry Wallace and a British war relief poster. He was named Artist Laureate by Delta Phi Delta, an honorary art fraternity, and received honorary degrees. His final paintings, *Spring in the Country* and *Spring in Town*, were done in his summer studio, an abandoned depot in Clear Lake, Iowa. He made the 15th black-and-white lithograph, *Family Doctor*, of the hands of his physician, Dr. A. W. Bennett of Iowa City.

Grant Wood's Washington High School yearbook staff, 1910. Grant is in the center, second row. His life-long friend, Artist Marvin Cone, is at the right in the front row.

FRESHMEN

SOPH  OMORE

JUNIOR

Illustrations by Grant Wood, the Washington High School yearbook, 1908, the Reveille.

1942 Grant Wood died of cancer at the University of Iowa Hospitals, February 12, the day before his 51st birthday. He was buried beside his mother at Riverside Cemetery in Anamosa, Iowa. Nan sold his Iowa City home in October. She and Ed attended the opening of the Memorial Exhibition at the Art Institute of Chicago and were entertained by Mrs. Potter Palmer, president of the board.

1949 Nan and Ed celebrated their Silver Wedding Anniversary with a trip to Catalina.

1951 Nan helped dedicate Grant Wood School in Cedar Rapids.

1955 Nan and Ed toured Portugal, North Africa and Italy. Nan unveiled the bronze plaque dedicating Grant's stained-glass *Memorial Window* in Cedar Rapids.

1957 Nan came from California to open "Grant Wood and the American Scene," a retrospective exhibit at the Davenport Municipal Art Gallery.

1958 The *American Gothic* couple appeared in "The Music Man" on Broadway.

1960 Nan and Ed took a trip around the world.

1964 Nan sold Grant's art and personal effects to the Davenport Municipal Art Gallery for $30,000.

1966 Wax figures of the *American Gothic* couple were unveiled at the Palace of Living Art in Buena Park, California.

1967 Ed Graham died July 3. Nan moved into a modest house he had bought in Riverside, California. Nan became an honorary director of the Palace of Living Art. She sued Johnny Carson and NBC, and *Playboy* and *Look* magazines for publishing defamatory versions of *American Gothic*. The cases were settled for an undisclosed amount.

1970 *Portrait of Nan* was exhibited at Expo '70 in Osaka, Japan.

1971 Nan appeared on the television show "To Tell The Truth."

1973 Nan attended the first Grant Wood Festival, Anamosa, Iowa.

1974 The house, near Anamosa where Nan and her brothers were born, burned October 3. The Gothic house in Eldon, Iowa, was designated a national monument.

1977 Nan sued *Hustler* magazine for publishing an obscene version of *American Gothic*, and the case was dismissed. Her biography appeared in *Who's Who of American Women*.

1979 Nan was guest of honor at Gothic Day in Eldon, Iowa, the site of the Gothic house.

1980 The United States Treasury issued a Grant Wood Gold Medallion. Nan wrote to the Zugs for advice about her book manuscript, *My Brother, Grant Wood*, commenting, "publishers take their time in replying."

1983 Nan attended the opening of an exhibit at the Whitney Museum featuring *American Gothic*, and made a television documentary about her brother. She said of the painting, "She's really become me."

1984 Her eyesight failing, she entered a Riverside, California nursing home.

1986 Nan donated scrapbooks about Grant, which she had worked on since the 30s, to the Davenport Museum of Art.

1988 Nan broke her hip and moved to LeHavre Convalescent Hospital. Her holiday message urged the issuance of a postage stamp to commemorate Grant Wood's 100th

birthday in 1991. (The U.S. Postal Service issued an Iowa commemorative stamp featuring Wood's *Young Corn* in 1996.)

1990 Nan died December 14, at the age of ninety-one.

1991 A memorial gathering for Nan Wood Graham preceded her burial in Riverside Cemetery, Anamosa, Iowa, February 13. She was buried beside her mother and brother.

Grant Wood stands by his completed painting, Midnight Ride of Paul Revere, *in 1932 at the Turner Alley Studio where he lived and worked from 1924–1932. With the exception of* American Gothic, *Grant posed with each of his major paintings, after completion, to insure his copyrights. The Metropolitan Museum of Art owns this painting.*

#5 Turner Alley
Grant Wood's famous studio

This door from Grant Wood's studio is in the collection of the Cedar Rapids Museum of Art.

Below: Exterior of the Turner Mortuary carriage house, 800 Second Avenue SE, Cedar Rapids, Iowa, where Grant Wood had a second floor studio and home for himself, his sister and mother for a decade until 1933, when he moved to Iowa City to join the University of Iowa art faculty.

The interior of Grant Wood's studio at #5 Turner Alley in Cedar Rapids, Iowa, where he lived with his mother Hattie and sister Nan when he painted American Gothic *in 1930. Mrs. Wood braided the rug seen in the compact studio.*

William A. Kittredge, friend of Grant Wood and Director of Design and Typography, Lakeside Press, Chicago, said of Wood's #5 Turner Alley studio in Cedar Rapids:

"The combined living room and studio was arranged also to be used by a company of amateur players for the presentation of amateur theatricals. Flowers and plants in profusion brought the outdoors—nature—into the apartment. It was always so, wherever Grant lived. One day when his mother was ill in bed, Grant took me in to see her, and I was impressed by the peaceful quiet of this Quaker lady in a room of pine, the principal decoration of which was Mason jars of preserved fruits and vegetables of the country, set in a row along a window ledge against the light. It struck me at once how beautiful these things are in reality, and how to this pioneer woman they must be infinitely more significant."

No space was wasted. At right of the fire-place, the doors opened for the dish cupboard and a folding table. Nan called this "Mother's hot dog stand."

Winnifred Cone, model for Grant Wood's *Fruits of Iowa* and widow of painter and lifelong friend of Grant Wood, Marvin Cone, said: "I remember one funny episode. Grant asked me to come and pose for one of those figures for the Montrose Hotel murals. They're at Coe College now in the library. It was my most embarrassing moment—I fainted. I was holding Mrs. Wood's sewing basket instead of cabbage, and something in the other hand, and this bright light—Grant used lights a lot—this bright light was shining on me, and so I just fainted dead away. And I was so embar-rassed. And Mrs. Wood was running around trying to comfort me. But Grant—the nicest thing about Grant—he never batted an eye; he just went right on drawing."

Wood Family Fortitude

Eight years younger than her brother Grant, who was born in 1891, Nan Wood and two other brothers, John and Frank, completed Hattie Weaver Wood's family.

Nan was always quick to correct the frequent impression that the Wood children came from an extremely poor background, saying:

"This simply is not true, Grandfather Weaver, my mother's father, was a well-to-do sheriff of Linn County, while Grandfather Wood was a prosperous farmer. Our father built a nice home for his bride on the farm near Anamosa. He prospered by farming this rich Iowa land, and during his short lifetime, completely paid off the mortgage. There were no debts of any kind.

..."Grant was ten and I was sixteen months old when Father died. In the spring, Mother sold the farm, and we went to town where her father was in the automobile business. She invested in a house on 14th Street, not far from Coe College. All that Mother had were the proceeds from the sale of the farm, part of which went toward the purchase of the house, and a small amount of insurance money.

"I am a believer in fate. Had our father lived, he undoubtedly would have become a rich Iowa farmer, and Grant would have most likely followed in his footsteps. His great talent would have been lost to the world."

She remembered many periods of difficult circumstances for the family, but despite these apparent hardships, Nan remembers these years with fondness. They held a promise of things to come as they watched the young artist in their midst develop and perfect his talent. ..."Mother always said Grant was born under a lucky star and would go far. I guess the three of us knew that someday he would make his mark in the world."

Nan, who became Mrs. Emmett Edward Graham in 1924, started her first scrapbook of newspaper and magazine clippings and other memorabilia about her brother in the early 30s. Over the years, she assembled more than thirteen volumes, which are now in the collection of the Davenport Art Museum. These, combined with her vivid recollections, relate a nostalgic journey of devotion, endurance and fortitude.

1929 oil on upson board, 20-1/2 x 17-7/8 inches

Woman with Plant(s)

© Cedar Rapids Museum of Art Collection

William A. Shirer, writer from Cedar Rapids and Coe College graduate, wrote in his *20th Century Journey,* Simon and Schuster, 1976:

"...the mother [Hattie Weaver Wood] moved to Cedar Rapids with her four children and, with part of the five-thousand dollars left from the sale of the farm, bought a modest house not far from us on 14th Street. She was the inspiration of Grant's life—and in a way—mine. It was in her that I first grasped the wonder and the beauty of human fortitude, of how a human being could survive degrading poverty, and the numbing heartbreaks and hardships that went with it with grace and dignity. Like her son, she refused to be defeated by what life at its worst had brought her. All this Wood has preserved for posterity in his painting of her, *Woman with Plant(s),* a copy of which hangs before me now in my study. It is one of the great portraits painted in our time. Wood thought it was his most enduring work."

Fire in the Studio, Winter, 1932

Front page, January 14, 1932 edition of The Gazette

Fire Damages Local Artist's Studio Home
Mrs. Graham Burned as Two Assist Mother to Escape;
Believe Painting Not Hurt

"Fire which broke out at 10:30 a.m. today in a storeroom at the top of the stairs leading into Grant Wood's attic studio in Turner alley just missed being a tragedy.

"Mr. Wood suffered bad burns on his right arm and hand and the right side of his face when he opened the door of the storeroom to discover what was causing a crackling noise and the flames burst out into the room. His sister, Nan Wood Graham, was also burned about the face while assisting their mother, Mrs. Hattie B. Wood, down the narrow passageway into which the flames were fast forcing their way and which was their only means of escape. Defective wiring is thought to have caused the fire."

Amana Friends Lend a Hand

Nan Wood Graham recalled the generosity of their Amana friends after the studio fire. She noted that many times their gifts of canned goods, fresh eggs, cabbage and other garden produce helped wonderfully with the food bill in a time of great need. In turn the landscape of the Amana Colonies, which inspired many of Grant Wood's paintings, is immortalized in his work.

In a 1996 edition of *Willkommen*, **Peter Hoehnle** notes:

"In 1928, Wood's relationship with Amana deepened. That year Carl Flick, a young clerk at the West Amana General Store, was confined to his house when part of his face became paralyzed due to exposure while hunting. To fill the time, Flick began to copy pictures. …Flick wrote Grant Wood a letter asking questions about brushes and paints. Wood just appeared one day. …He recognized that Flick had great natural ability and began to take him along on sketching trips. Wood made a point of promoting Flick's work. …the artist brought his own family to the Amanas, where his elderly mother, Hattie, enjoyed buying goat's milk. …and his sister, Nan, was remembered as being friendly and for dressing in the latest fashions."

Paintings and Values

The late Mrs. Arthur Collins of Cedar Rapids and Dallas, Texas, recalled in the 1960s that when her mother-in-law in the 1930s had an opportunity to select from two paintings of similar views of nature, one by Grant Wood and one by Carl Flick, she purchased the Flick. In the 1990s, with Grant Wood paintings and prints selling for thousands of dollars, collectors have turned to purchasing works by students of Grant Wood. A number of his students went on to distinguished careers including the late Conger Metcalf of Boston, John and Isabel Bloom, Davenport, Iowa, and Lee Allen of Iowa City.

One Artist Per Family?

Nan Wood Graham said she was brought up with the smell of turpentine. When brother Grant wasn't using it for his painting, their mother was doctoring them with it, using it for disinfectant and poultices. Eventually, Nan would take a brush in hand, but her first art experience was drawing with Grant.

"I learned that his enthusiasm was catching," she said. "Always patient, he would show me what to do, but he would never touch the work of a student. He'd say, 'If I did, it wouldn't be your work.'"

He taught by demonstration, drawing on the back of an envelope and saying, "Now draw it yourself."

Nan begged Grant to color her picture of a room interior for a furniture company's coloring contest, but no matter how hard she coaxed, he refused. "You've got to be honest about this," he told her. She took his advice and won a miniature wood-burning cook stove.

She recalled, "When I went downtown to claim the stove, I became so excited that I started to faint. I ran outside the store, lay down in the snow, and when I came to, I was too ashamed to go back inside the store. The stove was delivered to our house by truck, and for a while, I was the envy of all the girls in the neighborhood."

When she showed interest in art, her Aunt Sallie told her, "One artist in the family is enough." Years later, Nan said, "I believe in destiny." She did not believe that hers was to be an artist. Asked what her life might have been had she not been Grant Wood's sister, she said, "I probably would have been a farmer's wife, but Grant would still have been Grant."

Her teachers said she was quick to learn and original in her ideas. She also enjoyed taking off on one of her brother's most famous ideas, *American Gothic,* creating her own version of the Gothic couple in the artist's company. The only oil painting she ever created, *Boarding House Bath,* was a composition of period plumbing fixtures and two roomers peeking to see if anyone was in the bathroom. Her brother had planned to paint "the bath-1880" with a man in red flannel underwear, but his search for the red flannels brought accusations of publicity-seeking, and he never did the painting. Perhaps Nan thought somebody in the family had to do it. Her painting now belongs to the State Historical Society of Iowa, given by Joan Liffring-Zug Bourret.

Somewhere along the line, she learned the difficult technique of reverse painting on glass, but the pieces she created were stored in the attic until Sara, Grant's wife, discovered them and said they should be exhibited. They were shown in New York City in 1938.

While a patient at the Oakdale Sanitarium in 1929, Nan learned leather tooling. She developed a prize-winning technique, and Grant wanted her to teach it at his Stone City Art Colony in the summer of 1932. However, Ed was recuperating from an automobile accident in Albuquerque, and she felt she should be with him. "I always felt I let Grant down by not staying and teaching," she said. "He was disappointed. I also missed a colorful period in my brother's life."

The Iowa Stethoscope, Oakdale Sanitarium's newsletter, noted: "Many of you will remember that she first became interested in this work while assisting in our O.T. shop, and she gives Oakdale credit for starting her in this pleasant work."

Nan and Ed were having a hard time making it in California in 1939, and Grant worked out a way to help them. He wired train fare for Nan to come to Iowa City, and then taught her how to color his lithographs of fruits and flowers. As Grant mixed tube watercolors, Nan numbered the jars and made notes, and she was "totally amazed at the large number of green shades that could be created." She went home and taught Ed, and together they colored Grant's lithographs. Ed did the greens and she did the other colors. At first, she sent the prints to Grant for checking, but they became so skilled that he soon said, "There is no need whatsoever of my checking them anymore."

Associated American Artists sold the colored prints for $10 each, and for about three years the Grahams received a monthly check of $100. It was, Nan said, "a lifesaver."

The relative who discouraged Nan from becoming an artist must have had quite an impact on her. Decades later, someone asked about her own talent, and she said, "All I ever paint are my walls and my face."

Somehow, one feels, she could have painted more than that.

Nan's Art Works

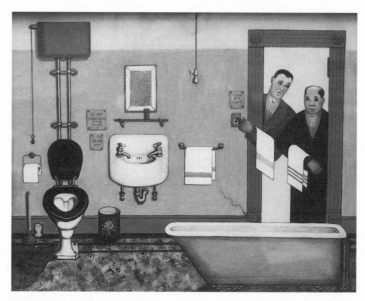

Boarding House Bath, *oil painting. Inspired by Nan's early years in California. Gift to the State Historical Society of Iowa from Joan Liffring-Zug Bourret.*

Dachshund on Roller Skates, *reverse painting on glass. Gift to the Cedar Rapids School District from Fran Rankin Price.*

Nan's Art Stays with the House

Dr. Pauline Moore purchased Grant Wood's home on East Court Street, Iowa City, in 1942, from Nan Wood Graham after Wood's death. Two reverse glass paintings signed by Nan Wood were left in the attic of the home.

The Hunted

The Catch

The Hunted and The Catch *were inherited by Dr. Moore's daughter, Maria Miltner Stender, in 1992. They are now in the collection of Bill Bilsland III, art and antique dealer of Cedar Rapids, Iowa, and California. Bill often lends his Grant Wood collection for display at the Annual Grant Wood Festival held at Stone City, Iowa.*

Side-by-Side

When Grant Wood was fifteen, he won the bid to paint Central Park Presbyterian Church in Cedar Rapids, and Nan, whom he called "Nicky," was his barefoot, pigtailed assistant.

"He had the low bid—twenty-five dollars—and it cost him almost that for lumber and scaffolding," she said. "I helped him mix the paint. It was calcimine, and I squeezed out the lumps. Grant would make the stencil, and I would hold it for him.

"Grant continued his interior decorating business intermittently for more than twenty years—until well after *American Gothic*. Grant took the upper part of the room and I took the lower. He showed me how to hold the brush and how not to leave brush marks. He designed and made his own stencils for borders. In all his work, he was a perfectionist, and we worked up a good reputation as decorators, plying our trade in some fine homes."

She remembered his first art sale as an unhappy experience. "The Ladies Aid of our church got together to produce a cookbook, and an elder of the church proposed that Grant paint something on the cover of each of the 100 books. Grant was promised one dollar for the lot. He put his whole heart into it, painting each cover in watercolor with utmost care.

"When the time came to receive payment, the elder put Grant off with, 'Some other day.' When my brother approached the man a second time, the elder stomped his cane on the ground and said, 'What dollar? Such effrontery!'"

She recalled that Grant did receive five dollars for an oil painting of the palisades along the Cedar River from the mother of his friend, Donald Barry.

Nan said, "When I was a little kid, most of the girls in Grant's drawings were me."

She was jealous of Grant's artist friend, Marvin Cone, who took her brother away to go on sketching trips. However, when Marvin couldn't go, Nan was permitted to accompany Grant to Cedar Lake.

Remarking on her brother's concern with authenticity, she said, "When he was a child on the way to country school, he observed grasshoppers, caterpillars, snakes, frogs and the like and occasionally adopted them as pets. This patient examination of everything around him was important; for in later years, he remembered every little detail.

Antioch Country School near Anamosa, attended by Grant Wood, is a preserved historic site in the care of Jones County Supervisors.

"He was pursuing authenticity when he made masks of two friends by putting plaster on their faces. For breathing, he inserted one tube in one boy's nostril and another in the other's mouth. The masks turned out well, despite Mother's natural concern that the boys would smother."

They also kept strange pets, like the rooster that modeled for *Appraisal* and crowed at four a.m. daily. Nan thought the rooster might be lonesome and showed it its mirror image. "This was a mistake," she said. "He got red in the wattles, fluffed his feathers and wanted to fight. Furthermore, he started to crow, and it seemed he'd never stop. Grant said it was enough to wake the dead in the mortuary next door."

At eighteen, Grant wanted to go to art school but had no money for tuition. He peered longingly into a life-drawing classroom at the University of Iowa and saw an empty easel. He went to it and started to work. When the teacher asked for his admission card, he said he had forgotten it, and, Nan said, "The teacher was so impressed with

Grant's work that he 'forgot' to ask for the card again. Grant stayed for a year without being registered or paying."

Grant was a night person, Nan said. "Frequently he would arrive home late with some good news, poke his head into our bedroom and ask, 'Are you awake?' We always were by then, and he would sit on the edge of our bed and share his good fortune. Those midnight talks are some of my happiest memories."

Nan could identify the childhood memories that inspired her brother's work, even when she did not share them. Speaking of Grant's black-and-white lithograph, *Sultry Night,* his only art work of a frontal nude, she said, "When Grant was a boy on the farm, hired men were given no facilities. Nights, they slept in the hay. Baths were drawn from the watering trough after the sun had warmed the water all day long. The men carefully dipped buckets in the water to avoid stirring up the settlings in the bottom. Horses are very particular and won't drink water that isn't clean. The hard-working men looked forward to sultry nights as these were considered best for bathing."

Nan helped him in a painting experiment by playing "Song of India" over and over on the Victrola while Grant painted the colors the music evoked for him in a modernistic style.

While Grant was in Europe, Nan took extensive notes for him in a course on the Johonnett method of painting, which she studied in Cedar Rapids. Ralf Johonnett, from California, was an expert in color schemes.

Grant used the method to create a frieze of a tropical paradise for the school cafeteria, and while he later regretted the purple prose of the monologue he wrote to go with it, Nan said, "I liked his sentiments." Emma Grattan, art supervisor for the Cedar Rapids schools, said, "It's so strange. The one person who didn't take the Johonnett course teaches his methods better than anyone else."

At one point when Grant was too fat and Nan was too thin, he suggested that they change plates at the dinner table. That way, she would get fatter, and he would get thinner. She said, "Grant had sugar on his lettuce, sugar on his tomatoes, and sugar enough to fill half his coffee cup. He had butter on everything, including radishes, celery and cake. The sugar was like medicine to me, and Grant missed his sugar and butter. After a week, he decided he'd just as soon be fat. I would just as soon stay thin, so by mutual consent, we gave up the great experiment."

Nan posed for her brother when he created the design for the *Memorial Window* in the Cedar Rapids Coliseum wearing a dress of wet cotton jersey to get the proper drape. She represented a figure symbolizing peace, and she said, "Grant gave my face classical features, but the body is mine."

The window was not dedicated until 1955, thirteen years after Grant's death, and Nan came from California to unveil the plaque with her brother Frank from Waterloo.

When Nan lived with her mother and Grant, the door was never locked because Grant always forgot his keys. All kinds of strangers wandered in and looked around, some going as far as helping themselves to a piece of pie or a cup of coffee.

One Sunday when they had just sat down to Mrs. Wood's excellent dinner, Grant answered a knock at the door and a young man asked him to step outside for a private conversation. It went on for so long that Grant's dinner got cold, and he came in to report that the visitor claimed to be his son. He said Grant was working on the hotel murals in Waterloo when he met the mother. Since the murals were finished only three years earlier, Grant said, "You look pretty big for a three-year-old." He asked if the lad had blackmail in mind, and the fellow said, "No, I just thought it would be nice to have you for a father and come and live with you." He also asked if he could come up and watch Grant work once in awhile. Permission was granted, but he was never heard from again.

The friends Grant made during his Iowa City years included writer Christopher Morley, whom Nan admired greatly "because he was kind and humble despite his fame." She probably also appreciated his estimate of *American Gothic,* which was, "In those sad and yet fanatical faces may be read much of what is right and what is wrong with America. The man's somber eyes, tight lips and the knuckled hands on the pitchfork remind one of Oliver Cromwell. It seemed to me one of the most thrilling American paintings I had ever seen."

Nan said, "The Missouri artist Thomas Hart Benton also won my admiration for his kindness and his modesty. Also, he didn't know the meaning of fear. A small private plane he chartered had trouble in a snow storm and landed in the stubble of a corn field. Telling us about it later, Grant said the incident didn't faze Benton a bit."

In 1931, Nan was back to her old role as Grant's painting assistant, and they were turning his workshop into a bedroom for their ailing mother when Grant's future wife, Sara Maxon, dropped in. This was the first time Nan had seen Sara, and she was "dressed fit to kill." Sara wanted to help and asked for a paint brush, but Grant looked at her clothes and her manicured nails and refused to give her one.

Mr. and Mrs. Grant Wood in their Iowa City home. Married in 1935, Grant divorced Sara in 1939.

Sara and Nan did not become well-acquainted immediately, because Nan had to return to Albuquerque, where her husband was recuperating from an auto accident. Mrs. Wood had been out of the hospital for just four days when Nan had to leave. Sara took "wonderful care of Mother, making her comfortable in every way and bringing her books, magazines, and flowers" for the month Nan was away.

The day Nan returned, Sara took her for a ride in Grant's car and revealed their marriage plans. The next day, Grant said to his mother and sister, "Perhaps you've guessed it. Last night Sara and I decided to get married." He believed they were suited to each other because she was an actress and an operetta singer. They thought alike, he supposed, and, he added, "Best of all, she fits in with you two."

Mrs. Wood had misgivings about the union, but if Nan had any reservations, she said nothing at the time. She must have known that her close ties to Grant would be altered. If so, it was not for long. The 1935 marriage ended in 1939. Nan said, "The marriage had its happy moments, but eventually it turned into a traumatic nightmare for Grant, who came out of it shaken and hurt."

At the end of his rope, Grant said, "Nicky, do me a favor. Go to California and take her (Sara) with you. I'll be forever grateful."

Nan and Ed did just that, arriving in Los Angeles broke. Nan said, "Sara was not accustomed to eating at hamburger stands, and we ran out of money."

That's when Grant devised a new way for Nan to assist him—by coloring a set of lithographs, *Fruits, Vegetables, Wild Flowers,* and *Tame Flowers.* Now valued in the thousands of dollars, these were sold at the time by Associated American Artists in New York City for ten dollars each.

A spin-off from the lithographs was fabric printed with Grant Wood's *Midnight Ride of Paul Revere.* American Artists sent Nan enough material to make the bedroom drapes now in the Davenport Museum of Art collection, and she said, "An unexpected development was that people bought the fabric by the yard for framing."

Nan was in Grant's room at University Hospitals, Iowa City, for the last round of drinks her brother would share with his friends. The date was February 9, 1942, and he lapsed into a coma shortly thereafter. Nan could not force herself to go to his bedside, and she remembered that he had felt the same way about their dying mother. There were no last words. They would not be side-by-side again until February 13, 1991, when they would lie in Riverside Cemetery, Anamosa, with their mother.

Lithographer Grant Wood

Grant Wood hand colors one of the four different lithographs of a master set for Nan and Edward to follow when they colored the remaining 996 copies.

Grant working on a lithograph at his Iowa City home.

Photographs of Grant Wood in Iowa City from 1934 to 1941 are from Edwin B. Green, who worked at the Press Citizen *and often brought along a cameraman to photograph Grant Wood.*

"Other American artists made lithographs of the midwestern scene...Thomas Hart Benton and John Steuart Curry, but Grant Wood's are different, unique...Wood limited himself to the use of the lithograph crayon leaving out the rich textures that were available. ...He developed a method of short, crossing lines and also circular lines. ... He idealized his landscapes, removing the blemishes and showing his subjects at their best. He painted and drew the Iowa scene in a way that nobody else has."

—Gustav von Groschwitz, former curator and associate director, University of Iowa Museum of Art

The Four Color Lithographs
Hand-colored by Nan and Edward Graham

Wild Flowers
1938 lithograph, 7"x10"
Collection of the Davenport Museum of Art

Tame Flowers

1938 lithograph, 7"x10"
Collection of the Davenport Museum of Art

Fruits

1938 lithograph, 7"x10"
Collection of the Davenport Museum of Art

Vegetables

1938 lithograph, 7"x10"
Collection of the Davenport Museum of Art

Black-and-White Lithographs Autographed to Nan and Edward Graham

December Afternoon

1941, 8-7/8 x 11-7/8 inches. Collection of the Davenport Museum of Art

Autographed: "To Nan and Edward from their brother Grant Wood"

February

1941, 9 x 11-3/4 inches. Collection of the Davenport Museum of Art

Autographed: "To Nan & Ed, Much love and appreciation, Grant Wood"

July 15

1939, 9 x 12 inches. Collection of the Davenport Museum of Art

Autographed: "To Nan and Ed with love Grant Wood"

Approaching Storm

1940, 11-3/4 x 9 inches. Collection of the Davenport Museum of Art

Autographed: "To Nan and Ed Graham, Christmas, 1940, Grant Wood"

Photograph by Steve Ohrn, State Historical Society of Iowa

The American Gothic *house, Eldon, Iowa*

The Inspiration for Nan's Most Famous Pose

On a fine spring day in 1930, Grant Wood was driving through Wapello County in southern Iowa with one of his art students, John Sharp, when he spotted the house that would inspire his most famous painting, *American Gothic*. The small dwelling with a Gothic window above its front porch was in tiny Eldon, Sharp's hometown. Wood made a sketch on the back of an envelope and asked his student to photograph the house. At that time it was the home of Gideon and Mary Jones. Within a year, it became one of the best known images in the Iowa landscape.

The modest house was immortalized, along with the pair who stood in front of it in Grant Wood's imagination.

No one knows exactly when the house was built or by whom, but the land on which it stands was plotted in 1881 by W. H. Jacques.

Built of board and batten (strips of wood to cover cracks), it was referred to by an architect as "carpenter Gothic" or "steamboat Gothic." Perhaps its proximity to the Des Moines River influenced its style. At the turn of the century, the house was a candy and novelty shop. It belonged to a family named Dribble and then to the Joneses, who owned it when when Wood fell in love with it. Their grandson, Whitey Jones, operated the Jones Cafe and Rocket Room in Eldon with his wife, Mary, and he remembers waiting on Grant Wood and John Sharp at the restaurant in 1930.

The Gothic window on the second floor seems out of place in such a small house, and some have speculated that it came from a church somewhere. In any case, Grant Wood once told a reporter, "I had my sister in there and my dentist—both looking kind of stern to go with the building, which I made look halfway between a church and a house."

In the year Grant Wood died, 1942, the house was purchased by Seldon and Myra Smith from a family named Howard.

In 1945, Nan worked with a group trying to buy the Gothic house and preserve it, but that effort apparently came to nothing. By 1970, the house was described as "decaying," and a year later, it was vacant. A newspaper account said, "The grass grew up high during the summer; a woodpecker has pecked a hole in one of the porch columns, and vandals have broken out some of the windows now replaced with tin. Black roll roofing has been used to cover the curling shake shingles, and weather has turned the white paint a dull gray. Inside, the plaster has crumbled; pieces of faded wallpaper have cracked and fallen off."

Carol and Bill Wilkinson moved into the house in March 1977, with their dog Wimpy, who loved posing for pictures on the porch or looking out the windows. At that time, a bullet was found lodged in a bedroom wall. Their landlord was Carl Smith, the son of the couple who bought the house in 1942.

The Gothic house became a national monument in 1974, and in 1980, the 50th Anniversary of the painting of *American Gothic,* it was designated an Iowa Historical Site and entered in the National Register of Historic Places.

Carl Smith donated the house to the State Historical Society of Iowa in 1991, and it was officially dedicated as a State Historic Site on February 14 of that year. The following year the Society added a new roof, stabilized the porches, built a new foundation, installed mechanical systems including a fire-sprinkler, and landscaped the grounds.

A $150,000 project approved by the Iowa Legislature includes plans for an education center across the street to the south which will provide information on the life and art of Grant Wood and other regionalist artists, and exhibit *American Gothic* parodies.

The house, which is rented as a private residence, is not open to the public, but the exterior may be viewed.

Today, Wayne and Shirley Slycord, formerly of East Moline, Illinois, live next door to the Gothic house. When they built their retirement home, they considered giving it some Gothic touches, but Slycord says, "We didn't want to detract from the house Grant Wood painted.

"They have a lady who is the caretaker. I wouldn't mind being a caretaker there. They have a grant to build a park around the Gothic house, and they'll be having bus tours." ·

The Slycords have enjoyed the annual open house at the famous dwelling. He says, "The house has wooden floors, and you can barely stand up in the upstairs bedrooms. They have fixed it up nice on the inside with antiques."

The town of Eldon celebrates Gothic Days in June with a parade and all kinds of festive activity. The Gothic house is its claim to fame. At one time that claim was challenged by Roseanne Barr, the star of the television series "Roseanne," who, with her former husband and native Iowan Tom Arnold, opened a "loose-meat" restaurant in Eldon. That venture was short-lived, and the restaurant property was given to Indian Hills Community College.

Wayne Slycord says he's surprised at how many people come to take pictures of the house. "And they're real nice," he says, "not riff-raff. I was standing by our mailbox one day, and a lady stopped and asked if I had a pitchfork. When I work around the place, I usually wear my bibbies, and people wave."

The spirits of the artist and his models will never leave Eldon's Gothic house.

July 19, 1980, Gothic Day Celebration
Nan Wood Graham and Carl Smith are shown in front of the American
Gothic *house at Eldon, Iowa, now owned by the State Historical Society of
Iowa. The house is on the National Register of Historic Places.*

Model for *American Gothic* painting says it saved her life from being drab

An Associated Press article in a Riverside, California newspaper, 53
years after Nan Wood Graham agreed to pose for *American Gothic,*
says: "Mrs. Graham, 83, says her brother wooed her into posing by
promising no one would recognize her. He was wrong. ...she admits
being stung at first by critics...but later she began to relish the attention...Mrs. Graham said the painting has always been misinter-
preted...her brother didn't intend to depict a married couple, but a
small-town father with his spinster daughter. The model didn't fit the
role—Nan was 30 and married when Wood sought her help. ...Mrs.
Graham says she didn't think the painted lady looked anything like
her when *American Gothic* was first displayed...But now she's
decided, 'we look a lot alike. She's really become me.'"

Why My Brother Painted
American Gothic

by Nan Wood Graham

Excerpts from Magazine Digest, *May, 1944*

This is the first time that the story of America's most popular painting has been told. Here it is in the words of the sister of Grant Wood, America's own artist. American Gothic *now hangs in the gallery of the Art Institute in Chicago. To date the Institute alone has sold 22,000 reproductions of the painting. In addition, many thousands of prints have been sold by other organizations. The picture is familiar to millions for it has been reproduced in the picture sections of almost every American newspaper and magazine.* —Editors

One morning during the summer of 1930, my brother Grant Wood, Mother, and I calmly sat down to breakfast. This we had done many other mornings in our studio home that Grant had built in the attic of a barn located in the rear of the Turner Mortuary in Cedar Rapids, Iowa.

I have recalled this particular morning often, and distinctly remember that Grant, who usually appeared drowsy at breakfast because of his habit of painting half the night, seemed very much awake and had a broad smile on his face.

"Mom and Nicky," he said (Nicky being his pet name for me), "I have an idea for a painting that I think will do for the Chicago show." (By this he meant the Chicago Art Institute's Annual Exhibition of American Paintings.) "I think Dr. McKeeby (the family dentist) would be an ideal model for the man. He has a long narrow face. I have in mind a model for the woman, but I'm afraid she would be mad if I asked her to pose. Women want to look pretty, but I don't like to paint pretty women."

I spoke up. "What's the matter with me?"

Grant studied my face for a moment then exclaimed, "Why, yes. Of course, you'll do. You're sure you won't mind? Your face is too round, but I can stretch it out long, and you can omit the 'Iron Dog' (my marcel)."

Dr. McKeeby thought a great deal of Grant and Grant of him. In fact they were such good friends they once swapped a painting of a bridge for a bridge of teeth. Grant often referred to the transaction as a "bridge for a bridge." However, at first Dr. McKeeby was reluctant to pose. He agreed on the condition that the painting wouldn't look like him.

I had difficulty finding the rickrack trim for the dress. ...I was told such trimming was out-of-date. ...So I had to rip the rickrack off one of Mother's old dresses. (Later, when *American Gothic* became popular, the stores were full of rickrack and the late O. O. McIntyre, famous newspaper columnist, blamed the revival on Grant's painting.)

Grant selected one of Mother's dresses and I fixed myself up as he directed. I parted my hair in the middle and slicked it down flat. I wore the cameo pin which Mother also had worn when she posed for Grant's painting, *Woman With Plant(s)*. (Grant used this same cameo pin in a later painting, *Daughters of Revolution*.)

The actual painting of *American Gothic* took about three and a half months. I had to be on hand at all hours, for when Grant had a painting streak, he would paint all day long and way into the next morning. Grant painted Dr. McKeeby and me separately. We never posed together.

Finally the day came when *American Gothic* was finished. Grant crated it carefully and as he drove the last nail into the box, remarked to Mother and me: "I suppose it will be just my luck to have it rejected."

You can imagine our surprise and joy when word came that *American Gothic* had been accepted for the show and had won the coveted Norman Wait Harris Bronze Medal and $300. Mother, Grant and I joined hands and danced a jig.

As the world knows, the painting created a sensation; reproductions of it appeared in newspapers and magazines all over this country and in European publications. People flocked to the studio. We seldom had a moment to ourselves. People walked in without knocking, wandered around opening drawers and cupboards, asking questions and staring at us.

American Gothic was mistakenly titled *Iowa Farmer and His Wife* by some of the Iowa newspapers. This caused bedlam to break loose amongst Iowa farm wives.

The woman in the painting was called the "missing link," an "oddity." There were protests like: "Heaven help us if that's what an Iowa farmer's wife looks like." "That painting should be hung in a cheese factory; that woman's face would positively sour milk."

Strangely, no one took offense at the man in the painting. In general he was described as a "kindly sort of man" and "one in whom you could put your trust."

Grant was threatened with getting his head "bashed in" if he was not careful.

On the other hand, letters, telegrams and newspaper articles, extravagant in praise of *American Gothic,* kept pouring in from critics, art dealers, writers and people in all walks of life. Among the comments were "priceless," "untouched by foreign influence," "vitally significant," "authentic Americana."

In the *Saturday Review of Literature,* Christopher Morley wrote: "It is one of the most thrilling American paintings I have ever seen! In those sad and fanatical faces may be read much, both of what is right and what is wrong with America."

In answer to the fury of the farmers and their wives Grant said: "I simply invented some American Gothic people to stand in front of a house of this type. The people in *American Gothic* are not farmers but small-town people, as the shirt on the man indicates. My sister posed as the woman. She is supposed to be the man's daughter, not his wife. I hate to be misunderstood as I am a loyal Iowan and love my state."

When the farmers and their wives learned that I, Grant's own sister had posed for the painting, everything was all right. They were convinced he was not poking fun at them and meant nothing derogatory to Iowa farm life or farm people. They learned to love Grant's work and became his greatest fans, constantly sending him gifts of homemade cakes, jellies, and sausages.

There was a long waiting list of buyers for *American Gothic.* It was purchased by the Friends of American Art to become a part of the permanent collection of the Chicago Art Institute, at a price of $300. Today art experts have called it "priceless."

The painting has been on many tours all over America and Hawaii. It was the most popular painting at the Century of Progress Exposition. Thousands of reproductions and postcards of it have been sold. It is as popular among the plain people as it is with artists and critics.

Grant did not have the sort of start in life that might be expected to lead to iconoclasm. Like our two brothers, Frank and John, and myself, he was born on a farm near Anamosa, Iowa, our father being of Quaker descent, mother of Presbyterian. When Grant, the eldest of the family, was ten years old, Father died, and we moved to Cedar Rapids.

In Cedar Rapids, Grant's farm experience stood him in good stead. He milked cows, took care of horses and picked berries besides plowing and tending our own family garden. He was just as busy in the winter, shoveling snow, carrying ashes and helping in any way that would bring in some extra money. We had some mighty tough years, and Grant sacrificed a great deal to take care of Mother and me.

But, busy as he was at manual labor, he struggled to develop the gift for drawing that he had shown when very young. When he was fourteen, he won third prize in a national art contest for children of the United States and Canada, and this encouraged him—and us—a great deal.

The time came when he was able to attend summer school at the Arts and Crafts Guild in Minneapolis and later night school at the Chicago Art Institute. He also managed to put in a year at the University of Iowa. Then came the war and a spell in the Army. After discharge, he taught in the junior high school at Cedar Rapids for several years, but this job did not give him enough time to satisfy his yearning for paint. He jumped at the offer made by David Turner, a very good friend, of the use of a barn attic as a home and a studio. Here Mother and I lived happily, and Grant painted for long, earnest hours.

Daughters of Revolution, painted two years after *American Gothic,* caused almost as great a public sensation as the latter. Showing three dour, tea-drinking women standing in front of a reproduction of *Washington Crossing the Delaware,* it raised the ire of many of the Revolution's "Daughters" and "Sons." In San Francisco the Sons of the American Revolution* demanded its withdrawal from exhibition; an eastern woman said she would shoot Grant Wood. However, the DAR's of Iowa, with the exception of a few in Cedar Rapids, took the picture good-naturedly, having been broken in by the fuss over *American Gothic.* I was even asked to become a "Daughter."

Edward G. Robinson purchased the picture "to preserve his sense of humor," as he said. It was the most popular painting at the 1934 World's Fair in Chicago, and it has been shown in England.

Yet, in spite of the success his paintings enjoyed, Grant felt his greatest triumph was the home he made for us, which he designed and built with his own hands. From the way he talked in later years, I really believe he was prouder of that house than of anything else he did in his whole life.

Both Nan and Grant were eligible for membership in the Daughters and the Sons of the American Revolution.

Grant Wood remembered

Park Rinard, secretary to Grant Wood, wrote in 1972:

"At rare intervals in the generations of man, a creative artist emerges who can sum up in a single work of art the distinctive character of a nation—the fortitudes, the frailties, the fears and hopes, the loves and the sorrows that make them what they are. Such an artist was the creator of *American Gothic*. This is one reason his art is fresh and vigorous today."

Edwin B. Green, a former editor of the *Iowa City Press Citizen,* friend of Grant Wood and longstanding confidant of Nan Wood Graham, wrote for the retrospective:

"Through the Years with *American Gothic,*" University of Iowa Museum of Art, November 15, 1970–1971: "Many have tried to explain the long popularity of this painting and why it has remained so fresh and vigorous to so many people for forty years."

Perhaps the ultimate tribute came in 1966 from **Matthew Baigell,** then an assistant professor of art history at Ohio State University. In an article entitled, "Grant Wood Revisited," in the winter issue of the *Art Journal,* he wrote:

"*American Gothic* is probably the most famous American painting of the century. The fascination this work holds over people is in itself fascinating. Why, for example, do people invariably laugh when they either stand before it or see it in reproduction? Is it a laugh offered in nervous recognition of what they know is true about themselves but try so hard to repress? Do they see their self-portraits in middle age, or those of their neighbors? Wood seems to have painted an equivalent of their life and given them an image of what they may actually be. Certainly, there is the shock of recognition in those faces. Whatever else one may think of *American Gothic*—once seen, it is never forgotten."

Dr. Byron McKeeby, Grant Wood's dentist and model for *American Gothic,* said in 1935:

"He told me that he wanted a face showing integrity from a man with a sense of humor…who would not revel at the distortion that might be necessary to carry out his theme. The painting was in no manner intended to be a portrait."

Nan Wood Graham visited and posed with a replica of the American Gothic *couple at the Movieland Wax Museum in Buena Park, California, circa 1970s.*

The Many Guises of *American Gothic*

Edwin B. Green, managing editor of the *Press Citizen* in Iowa City in the 40s, bought two Grant Wood lithographs before he met the artist. The dealer who sold him the prints was surprised they did not know each other, and the next time he came to town, he introduced them. Green became a close friend of Grant and Nan, and he collected *American Gothic* parodies for forty years, giving his collection of more than 400 pieces to the Davenport Municipal Art Gallery in 1979.

Green found the first parody in a greeting card shop in 1938, and, he said, "It got to the point where I could walk into a store and be drawn to one as if it were a magnet."

The University of Iowa Museum mounted an exhibit, "Through the Years With *American Gothic*," November 15, 1970 through January 3, 1971, and Green wrote a time line for the catalog. In the 1940 to 1950 segment he wrote, "Even as art trends drastically changed in the U.S. in the 1940s and 1950s, *American Gothic* continued to intrigue the people. It became probably the most caricatured painting of all time, far exceeding the attention that had been give two other paintings, the *Mona Lisa* and Whistler's portrait of his mother."

He noted the opening tableau of "The Music Man," which hit Broadway December 19, 1957—"a take-off on *American Gothic* in the first scene, setting the mood for the entire show."

Continuing into the 1960s, he wrote, "The two figures in the painting were used over and over again by political cartoonists with the cartoons appearing through syndication in newspapers and magazines in every state. One lampoon of Lyndon Johnson, then President of the U.S., and his wife, Lady Bird Johnson, decorated the cover for a record album."

In 1961, the November issue of *The New Yorker* featured a Charles Addams cartoon depicting two Gothic characters walking down an art gallery corridor as if they had come alive and stepped out of the painting.

American Gothic became familiar to a third generation when children saw a Country Corn Flakes commercial featuring the Gothic couple on television, and in 1970 the fashion editor of the *New York Times* noted, "The American-Gothic hairdo—Grant Wood's heroine is it for '70."

The Gothic pair became flower people in 1970, and *Mad* magazine showed them with President Richard Nixon's head between theirs and his arms around their shoulders under the caption, "Silent Majority."

Green's collection continued to grow. Greeting cards abounded with images such as American-Gothic pilgrims with a turkey for Thanksgiving, two pink pigs for an anniversary, the farmer's daughter all alone saying, "Miss you!" and the pair as cats.

Political versions paired 1971 presidential candidates George Wallace and Shirley Chisholm in the pose; put gas masks on the couple to protest pollution; gave both of them black eyes; put money in the man's fist and had him say, "I'd rather fight than pay!" in connection with the refusal of Seventh Day Adventists to join a union; put Presidents Reagan, Nixon, Johnson, Carter, and Clinton with their wives into the picture as "just plain folks," and made Nan into a mule labeled "Congress," and Dr. McKeeby into Secretary of Agriculture Ezra Benson.

The Gothic pair became: George and Martha Washington; Liz Taylor and her husband Senator John Warner; Batman and Robin; scuba divers; formally-dressed opera-goers; the Folgers' lady and Mr. Clean; Bob Hope and designer Penelope McCormick; tourists in front of the *Arc de Triomphe*, and tourists in Hawaii enjoying "a vacation as American as pineapple pie."

Nan as Hayden Fry, University of Iowa football coach, and Dr. McKeeby as Tom Davis, basketball coach, was another representation, and Dick Smothers and Carol Burnett also became the couple.

One humorous calendar asked, "Whom [sic] are this famous couple? Circle one: Liz and Dick, Liz and Eddie, the Bobbsey Twins, Lewis and Clark, or Sears and Roebuck." The Gothic twosome posed with golf clubs and tennis racquets, as a Japanese couple, as Chinese in front of a pagoda, holding a toothpaste tube and brush, as Miss Piggy and Kermit the Frog, and as weight losers—she says, "Dieting is easy," and he says, "What's hard is not eating."

They have been portrayed as hoboes at Britt, Iowa, site of the world convention of kings of the road, chatting in front of a Gothic caboose; as Ragbrai cyclists preparing to ride across Iowa; as ballet dancers before an abstract Gothic arch, and as home remodelers with wallpaper and tools.

They blush deeply in a *Newsday* version that says, "Who says a tabloid has to be sensational?" Nan coughs painfully in an ad for Robitussin, and the two reverse roles as a feminist couple on a poster for New York's School of Visual Arts.

Samplings from the Edwin B. Green Collection
Davenport Museum of Art
A Parody of the American Spirit

The Environmental Change
VISTA United Nations Association
Vol. 7, No. 6, 1972

Margaret Fleming
American Artists Group, New York

A Look At The Man Liz Found
November 1976

A Revolutionary Plot
Horticulture, *December 1975*

Touting a Rocky Mountain vacation, Nan says, "Pa, I'm tired of hogs an' roosters an' apple pie." Another has Dr. McKeeby wearing earmuffs saying, "Our competition doesn't want to hear it. We'll give you a better deal on a Toyota anytime."

They advertised everything from jug wine to long distance service. Parodies appeared on bright blue bottles of Beam's Choice bourbon, on a skirt from Lord and Taylor portraying the couple as Minnie and Mickey Mouse, and on a plate by Howard Kottler in which Dr. McKeeby is twins, and Nan does not appear at all. They were on shopping bags from the Davenport Museum of Art, on napkins celebrating the 40th Anniversary of *American Gothic,* on bookmarks showing Nan winking, on countless calendars and as handmade dolls.

The Davenport Museum of Art showed parodies from the Green collection in conjunction with the 1996 exhibit, "Grant Wood: An American Master Revealed," and loaned 21 items to the Charles H. MacNider Museum in Mason City, Iowa, for an exhibition in 1997. Some of the parodies also are on display at the Grant Wood Tourism Center in Anamosa, Iowa.

Nan Wood Graham was interviewed by the *Des Moines Register* in November 1972, talking about her forty-two years of fame as the model for *American Gothic,* saying, "I have followed with interest and amusement the hundreds—maybe thousands—of cartoons and caricatures of *American Gothic* appearing everywhere from cereal boxes to *Mad* magazine in past years.

"I get a kick out of it when it is done in good taste. It's a left-handed compliment to Grant when done in good taste."

The guest bedroom of Nan's Riverside home was plastered with her own collection of parodies, including Liz Taylor and Senator John Warner, and the Beverly Hillbillies.

The reproduction of the original painting and its myriad spin-offs made Nan Wood Graham a woman of a thousand faces—at least.

Ed Green was the first to know of Grant Wood's death in February 1942, and he scooped his own paper to get the story on the wire. In gratitude, Nan gave him two family quilts made by women in the Wood family in Virginia in the mid-19th century. The two foremost collectors of *American Gothic* parodies remained friends for life.

Parodies decorate Nan's bedroom

View of Nan's dressing table and chest with the many American Gothic *parodies she collected.*

Grant Wood talks about *American Gothic*:

"There is satire in it but only as there is satire in any realistic statement. These are types of people I have known all my life. I tried to characterize them truthfully—to make them more like themselves than they were in actual life. They had their bad points, and I did not paint these under, but to me they were basically good and solid people.

Friends sent Nan many cards featuring parodies of American Gothic *and she taped them to her bedroom walls.*

"I had no idea of holding them up to ridicule. I imagined Gothic people with their faces stretched out long to go with the house. ...It was my intention later to do a Mission painting as a companion piece with Mission bungalow types standing in front of it. The accent then, of course, would be put on the horizontal instead of the vertical. ...Of course, all this discussion pro and con is flattering as it indicates an interest in what I am doing."

American Gothic and Frontier Roots

The Nebraska State Historical Society Collection has an 1880s photograph by S.D. Butcher showing the John Curry sod house near West Union, Nebraska. A farmer is pictured holding a pitchfork; the family dog, horses, and household objects complete the scene. Grant Wood was strongly interested in pioneer architecture and artifacts symbolic of the people he knew best, and incorporated many of these elements in *American Gothic*. When working with interior design and architecture in Cedar Rapids homes, and later in his own home in Iowa City, Grant Wood drew on his pioneer roots and background for styles and themes, and for his collection of antique dishes and furniture.

Nan displayed copies of Grant Wood's art works that she posed for on the wall above her bed: Portrait of Nan, *at right above; and below, the* stained-glass Memorial Window.

Disgraceful!

Although Grant Wood posed for a photograph in front of every subsequent painting to protect his creative claim, he failed to retain reproduction rights to *American Gothic*. More than a quarter of a century after his death, Nan went to court to protest the desecration of his most famous work.

After Johnny Carson exhibited a version of the painting with the woman in a scanty bikini bra on the "Tonight Show" in 1968, *Look* magazine published the image with the comment, "It's make-fun-of-the-classics time—an old routine—but Carson does it well."

Nan didn't think much of that routine, and she became even more incensed when *Playboy* magazine

Nan Wood Graham
Photo from the archives of the Cedar Rapids Museum of Art.

published a version with the woman hoisting a purple sweater to display a voluptuous bare bosom and a dimpled navel.

This offensive version was put together by Kelly Riordan, Champaign, Illinois, using a *Playboy* gate fold and a print of *American Gothic*. A *Playboy* editor commented, "A nice combination of the traditional and the contemporary, Kelly. We hope Dolly Read, our May 1966 Playmate, doesn't object to being deposed."

Nan began to receive anonymous and insulting phone calls, and she said, "I was ashamed to go to church for a month."

She sued NBC-TV and the two magazines for $3 million apiece, charging them with invasion of privacy and holding her up to ridicule and disgrace. She claimed the images were vile and obscene.

The *Los Angeles Times* of May 1, 1968, wrote, "The difference between having your picture painted by your brother and having your face used in a caricature is exactly $9 million."

Nan said, "It is my hope that this suit has accomplished creating a lot of interest in Grant by just being filed and getting such big publicity all over the country. People will think twice before desecrating not only Grant's paintings, but those of others as well." She also said, "If I win, a substantial amount will go to charity."

Letters to the editor ranged from comments like, "If some people really think that Nan Wood Graham posed for the bikini and topless versions, she should be happy to pay $9 million to Johnny Carson and *Playboy* in appreciation," to, "I don't blame you for suing because I think that painting is a treasure and not something for ridicule."

Although *Playboy, Look* and NBC said they did not know the model was still alive and did not intend to invade her privacy, they settled the suits out of court for an undisclosed amount. The case was legally flawed because Nan's lawyer failed to demand a retraction before suing, and the settlement was modest.

Hustler magazine did it again in April 1977, publishing a bare-breasted version of *American Gothic,* and Nan sued for $10 million, charging the magazine and its publisher, Larry Flynt, with defamation, invasion of privacy and libel.

Her attorney, John T. LaFollette, said *Hustler* could not claim ignorance of Mrs. Graham's existence, as the others had, considering national publicity on the older law suits.

Nan learned about the *Hustler* picture from Joan Liffring-Zug (Bourret) of Iowa City. A friend had shown the picture to Ms. Liffring-Zug's husband. Friends in California urged Nan not to look at it, but she said, "I insisted on seeing it because I thought I should know what was going on, but I was afraid I would have a heart attack when I saw it.

"I was so shocked at seeing the thing—I was offended and disgusted and emotionally upset. My brother was very moral and would not approve of what had been done to his painting. It makes me feel sick. I feel I have been dragged through the gutter."

The suit was brought, and Nan won the first round. *Hustler* countersued, contending that she and her attorney were improperly using the courts and news reports to force payment of damages. A Los Angeles judge threw out the *Hustler* suit.

The case dragged on until October 1981, when a California Superior Court Judge, Eli Chernow, ruled that the satirical version of *American Gothic* published by *Hustler* was not defamatory. He granted a summary judgment in the magazine's favor, a decision based on law rather than facts and without trial.

Even though she lost the *Hustler* suit, Nan believed the publicity would discourage future outrages of this sort. Also, it allayed her fear that people would believe she authorized the disgraceful parody.

Another scurrilous use of the painting cropped up in a Trivial Pursuit game in 1986. The question was, "What famed painting features a Gothic house that was actually a brothel?" The answer on the back of the card was *American Gothic*. Grant Wood experts everywhere were unable to verify such a fact. Nan was not amused, but she did not bring suit—possibly because a dollar from every sale of the game went to the Statue of Liberty/Ellis Island Restoration Foundation.

Defamation was not always the issue. When Hazel Brown, a classmate of Grant Wood and his friend, Marvin Cone, used color illustrations of Grant's works in her 1972 book, *Grant Wood and Marvin Cone,* without permission, Nan sued the publisher, Iowa State University Press. According to Joan Liffring-Zug Bourret, Nan said she was paid slightly more than $1,500, and the illustrations in question were omitted from later editions of the book. Nan also complained that corrections she made in the book's manuscript did not appear in the published work. Those corrections are now at the State Historical Society of Iowa.

In later years, Nan's rights were protected by VAGA (Visual Artists and Galleries Association, Inc.), which collected royalties for commercial reproductions of *American Gothic*.

Today, VAGA and the Art Institute of Chicago, which owns *American Gothic,* work together to monitor and authorize uses of the painting. And by the terms of Nan's will, various beneficiaries receive these royalties.

The Norman Wait Harris bronze medal awarded to Grant Wood in 1930 for his entry of American Gothic *in the Annual Exhibition of American Paintings at the Art Institute of Chicago.*

Collection of the Davenport Museum of Art

Nan's Approvals

A November 12, 1972 issue of the *Des Moines Sunday Register* reports from an interview with Nan Wood Graham:

"She said she has followed with interest and amusement the hundreds—maybe thousands—of cartoons and caricatures of *American Gothic,* appearing everywhere from cereal boxes to *Mad* magazine… 'I get a kick out of it when it is done in good taste,' she said. 'It is a left-handed compliment to Grant when done in good taste.'"

The December 8, 1980 issue of *Newsweek,* **reported:**

"Graham…says she gets a kick out of most of the 'Gothic' spoofs. Her favorite is a California insurance company ad that shows the plain and unsmiling couple holding a baby. The caption reads: 'Life is full of little surprises.'"

Joan Liffring-Zug Bourret photo

Nan approved and assisted with the subjects for the Grant Wood golden-color collector's plates designed and created by Judy Sutcliffe, Audubon, Iowa, in her Greentree Pottery. From left are: Grant's Studio, *1971;* Antioch School, *1972, and* Grant Sketching, *1973. The plates were designed and sold to raise funds for the Grant Wood Festival.*

Whimsical Observations

Nan Wood Graham would most likely approve of this recent parody crafted for the cover of Richard Lord Acton's book released in 1998 by Iowa State University Press. Since his marriage in 1988 to Patricia Nassif of Cedar Rapids, Richard Lord Acton is a part-time Iowa resident, member of the British House of Lords, barrister of London's Inner Temple, former senior law officer in Zimbabwe, historian, and writer. Much of his American life is spent writing historical studies and whimsical observations of the worlds around him.

Photos by Joan Liffring-Zug Bourret

Nan Wood Graham designed many of her own clothes, showing her artistic talent. When she wanted to be an artist, she was told to learn to type. She is shown above in 1976 seated by the front door in her Riverside, California home with a reproduction of American Gothic. A gold cord hangs above the painting. The photographer is  reflected in a wall of glass rectangles at the left.

When not wearing a silver wig in later years, Nan wore one of her many hats. Shown wearing a favorite at a 1978 Iowa City Public Library reception, she is seen with Miriam Canter who attended the children's classes in 1932–1933 at Grant Wood's Stone City Art Colony.

July 17, 1980. Nan has her final look at American Gothic *at a retrospective of Grant's work in Chicago.*

Press release photograph courtesy The Art Institute of Chicago. From the Cedar Rapids Museum of Art Archives.

License Plate

American Gothic *collectors' stamp, cancelled Eldon, Iowa.*

Portrait of Nan

Nan Wood Graham once said, "It makes me very humble to think that of all the paintings Grant ever did, my portrait was the only painting he had in his home."

That portrait was a pay-back for his sister's willingness to pose as the dour young woman in *American Gothic*. She agreed to that because Grant promised that no one would recognize her, but he was wrong.

For the portrait, she was allowed to marcel her blonde hair in the fashion of the period and wear make-up. He wanted her to wear a white sleeveless blouse with huge black dots, and because such a garment could not be found, he dipped slices of raw potato in ink and printed his own fabric. Nan sewed the blouse. This wasn't the first time she had sewn for art's sake. The rickrack-edged apron in *American Gothic* was of her making.

Why the baby chick and the plum? Nan had been to town on the bus on a cold day before Easter and purchased the chick at the dime-store. She pulled it out of her pocket to show Grant, and he was enchanted with it for the purposes of his composition. It repeated the color of her hair. Feeling the pangs of hunger after her expedition, she found a plum to munch, and he was equally excited about that. Its color repeated the shade of the painting's background.

Nan named the chick "Louse," and it grew up at #5 Turner Alley. Nan said, "It thought it was a person and kept the same hours we did. Grant had a rubber cigarette that he would put with the real thing and offer to guests. One day somebody chose that one and dropped it on the floor. The chicken grabbed it and ran all around the room. From then on, Grant told guests, 'We have this chicken that loves cigarettes,' and he dropped the rubber one on the floor. One day Louse swallowed the whole thing, and I started to cry. I thought the chick was a goner, but it survived, and every time it saw Grant light up, it would make little coaxing sounds."

Nan was pleased with her likeness and that of Louse, but Chicago critic Emily Genauer had this to say about the painting: "*Portrait of Nan* is of a young blonde woman dressed in cheap finery and holding a baby chick in one hand and a piece of fruit in the other. Dexterously composed in a manner obviously derived from American folk painting (an effect emphasized by the looped-back drapery and oval frame), the subject has been endowed by the artist with all the

Portrait of Nan, *oil on masonite, 30 x 40 inch oval*

Portrait of Nan *painted in 1933, hung above the fireplace in Grant's Iowa City living room.*

bigotry, stupidity, malice, and ignorance which are rife in the provinces and are Wood's special target."

Nan's mild response was, "Wrong interpretation. She thought it was a satire."

The painting hung above the fireplace in Grant Wood's Iowa City home until his death, and he willed it to Nan. Eventually, she sold it for $10,000 to the Encyclopedia Britannica Collection, which auctioned it in 1952. The buyer, William Benton, was an executive of the company, and the portrait has been on extended loan to the Elvehjem Museum of Art, University of Wisconsin-Madison. The painting was exhibited at Expo '70 in Osaka, Japan, in 1970, because the Art Institute of Chicago would not lend *American Gothic* for the exposition.

Nicky, as Grant called her, was in her prime when this portrait was painted, and he gave back to her the rounded cheeks he deprived her of in *American Gothic*.

The portrait was one of the highlights of "Grant Wood: An American Master Revealed," a traveling exhibition mounted by the Davenport Museum of Art.

Grant Wood and Nan are shown in the living room of his Iowa City home in the 1930s. Nan is sitting on a lounge chair designed by Grant. The chair was commercially produced and sold.

Nan's Other Major Pose

Memorial Window, *1927–1929*

Stained-glass, 24 x 20 feet. Cedar Rapids Veterans Memorial Building, May's Island

Nan posed as the figure representing the Republic. Grant added a classical Grecian face to her figure holding a branch of peace and the laurel wreath of victory.

Grant Wood and portraits

From a University of Iowa taped interview with Nan Wood Graham. When asked if Grant Wood was really crazy about doing portraits, Nan recounted:

"Well, there was a man that brought in two photographs, one of his mother as a young woman and one as an elderly woman. He said to Grant, 'Use the one you want.' So Grant said, 'Well, she's just not a dowager to me, so I'll paint her like a young woman.' She had a Victorian dress, you know, with the buttons and so forth, and it was real quaint, and he finished it—it was an oval, ... and it was just beautiful. The man looked at it and said, 'I don't like it. I don't remember my mother...I wasn't born then. ...I want a painting of her when she was old.' So Grant put it in the storeroom, and when we had the fire, it burned up. And he had spent three months on it. ...

"That about wound up his doing portraits, except for the one of the little boy in the plaid sweater. ...This man wanted him to paint his boy. And in order to get out of it, Grant said it would be $600, and thought the man would leave. (He had previously charged just $300.) Instead, the man said, 'Okay, go ahead.' And then to make it tougher, Grant said, 'You'll have to let me pick out his clothes; I don't want him to look like little Lord Fauntleroy and then hate me the rest of his life.' So he said, 'I want to look at his background.' So Grant went to Clinton and the boy came in—he'd been playing ball—Grant said, 'That's it. I want to paint him that way.' So he did, and they were very pleased with it."

Photo courtesy University of Iowa Museum of Art, 1931 oil on masonite, 29-1/2 x 24-1/8 inches

Plaid Sweater

Gift of Melvin R. and Carole Blumberg, and Edwin B. Green through the University of Iowa Foundation.

The Weaver family, Cedar Rapids, Iowa, early 1900s. Grant Wood later used Great Aunt Matilda Peet, shown top left, as the model for the portrait Victorian Survival. Seated immediately below Aunt Matilda are the Woods (left, second row from top): Frank, Grant, John and Hattie Weaver Wood holding baby Nan on her lap. Nan gave this photograph to John Fitzpatrick.

Victorian Survival

Left: The 1931 painting, Victorian Survival, *is in the collection of Iowa's Dubuque Carnegie-Stout Public Library and on permanent loan to the Dubuque Museum of Art. Grant Wood drew inspiration for this work from a daguerreotype of Matilda now in the Davenport Museum of Art Collection.*

Nan's Life with Ed

The man who wooed and won Nan Wood had his work cut out for him. She undoubtedly measured him by her brother Grant, who was everything to her—father, brother and friend.

Ed Graham was twenty-eight and she was twenty-four when a mutual friend introduced them in downtown Cedar Rapids. Edward Emmett Graham was a World War I Navy veteran from Macon, Georgia, and he worked in the railroad shops of the Rock Island Line in Cedar Rapids. Their marriage in the courthouse at Marion, Iowa, 1924, was a surprise to their friends.

Because of Ed's job, they got free railroad passes, and, Nan said, "We could go most anywhere."

When someone asked her why she hadn't married an artistic type, she said it was because they couldn't get railroad passes, and she liked to get around.

Ed had a number of secrets, and the first was revealed when Nan coughed blood. He said, "Not you, too!" It was then that Nan learned that Ed's first wife, the mother of his three children, had died from tuberculosis. She had been a teenage volunteer in the hospital where Ed had been treated for the disease. They met, married and soon shared the dread disease. His children, two girls and a boy, were placed in foster homes.

Nan said, "In those days if you had TB, and if you had kids, it was sure death. He put the kids in foster homes, and they were resentful and terribly mad about that. They blamed him and blamed me, too. I didn't meet them until after Grant died. We kept them a secret. No one knew but my mother."

Nan went to Oakdale, a sanitarium for tuberculosis patients operated by the University of Iowa hospitals. "Ed applied for a job as a plumber in Iowa City to be near me, but he didn't know anything about plumbing. After working for two days, he developed a terrible cough and went to the doctor saying he had the flu. The doctor told me Ed had advanced TB. He was put in the hospital too, and we both stayed a year."

Nan never told her mother that she had tuberculosis, and Grant told Mrs. Wood that Nan was at Oakdale because of "throat trouble."

Because they caught it in the early stages, Nan's case was cured, and she was not contagious. Ed, however, needed more treatment, so they went to the Veteran's Hospital, Fort Bayard, New Mexico.

Uncle Clarence Wood gave her the money for the trip, and she stayed at the Red Cross while Ed was in the hospital.

The place was isolated, but, she said, "It was like being in a luxury hotel. We had the best food. The men would shoot deer, and we had everything."

Ed was restless, however. "He was a wanderer and never stayed any place long. He was not over TB, and he was always leaving the hospital against the advice of his doctors."

Money probably had something to do with it. His tuberculosis was ruled unconnected to his Navy service.

The Grahams thought they could make a living operating a rooming house, but the roomers didn't pay. They gave it up, and Ed went back to the hospital while Nan returned to Cedar Rapids to live with her mother and Grant at #5 Turner Alley for a year.

"Then Ed came back, and we moved to a rooming house," Nan said. "The landlady and her husband had battles, and the roomers would crawl out into the hall in their nightgowns to listen to the fight. Once a mouse ran between them, and a woman grabbed a broom, yelling 'I'll kill you!' The landlords stopped fighting, and the excitement was over. Everybody went back to bed."

Nan was scheduled to teach leather tooling at Grant's Stone City Art Colony in the summer of 1932, but Ed, who had returned to New Mexico, was hit by a car and Nan hurried there to care for him. She was always wistful about that missed opportunity.

For a time, Nan and Ed had a hamburger stand in Albuquerque, and Nan said, "I ran it. Sometimes we cleared $15 in a week and thought it was wonderful. We ate the leftover hamburger and stuff we handled, and I got fat on pastry. Ed was pleased and tried to help keep me fat by making me drink milk. He was afraid I might get TB again. But I was always allergic to milk and had bad sinus as long as I drank it. We didn't stay in the hamburger stand for very long. We sold out and went to California."

They lived from hand-to-mouth. Ed would buy a filling station, keep it for a few months and then sell it for several hundred dollars. Nan said, "We lived on that and what Grant sent us until we could save enough for another gas station and hold it for two months.

"Some places we lived two or three months, but sometimes we moved sooner. All we had was a suitcase. We stayed in some places for two weeks, and then Ed would say he couldn't stand it, and maybe we would move across the street, and that would be worse. I would clean and sterilize the place; we would pay a month's rent, and then Ed would send me to get it back. If I didn't get it all, he'd say, 'You have to go back. If it were a man, I'd do it, but this is a landlady. When we deal with a woman, it's your job.'"

Nan dreaded moving, knowing there would be a fight with the landlady in two weeks. They changed addresses so often that their whereabouts was unknown most of the time, and those addresses filled an entire book. Nan held no grudge against the landladies, apparently. She once gave a luncheon at which all the guests were former landladies.

This routine continued with Ed buying a house and selling it immediately for a small profit. When he bought a corner with a gas station, barbershop and apartments, the sale was more difficult, and they stayed there for a year.

A judge in Denver advised Ed that he must allow someone to adopt his children because it was unfair for them to be shuffled around to foster homes. He cried, but he agreed to give them up. The girls, Pauline and Lillian, stayed together, and the boy, Emmett, went to a different home.

"Ed went to see the boy once," Nan said. "The woman had been his foster parent before adopting him. He was an awfully cute kid with curls and brown eyes, and when he looked from Ed to his adoptive father, he said, 'I look more like Uncle Emmett.' His adoptive mother told Ed, 'I don't want you to come back here.'"

To distract him from the boy, the adoptive father told Ed where the daughters were, and this caused Nan some worry. She said, "Ed did a very dangerous thing. He would go to the school and try to pick out the girls among the children. He wouldn't speak—just look—but I was afraid they might think he was a child molester."

The Grahams returned to Cedar Rapids from California to care for Nan's Uncle Clarence soon after Grant's marriage to Sara Maxon. However, Clarence Wood made them buy all the groceries and asked them to lay in coal for the winter. Because they had no money, they told him they'd have to leave. Off they went in their panel truck fitted with a mattress, canvas water bags and an oil stove.

"We set out to see the world," Nan said, "and Grant asked what we were going to do for money. I said we could get a job, but I knew we couldn't do that because of the Depression. We trusted to luck."

They went East, taking the trip Clarence and Sallie Wood had promised Nan before her marriage—a trip that never happened. "We went to Washington and saw the country," Nan said. "Gas was cheaper than rent."

Because Nan's mother was ailing, they pre-arranged places to pick up mail, and Nan received three telegrams—in reverse order—in Virginia. The third gave information on Hattie Wood's funeral, the second said she had died, and the first said, "Mother is very low. Come home at once."

When Nan began to cry, Ed said, "Quit that crying. You are not going to cry. I'm not crying when my mother dies, and you're not crying when your mother dies."

She obeyed her husband, even though, she said, "I had an awful time controlling myself."

Grant sent her the money to come home, and Ed went to Macon, Georgia, to visit his mother.

When they returned to California and a new round of "cheap rooming houses full of nuts and cuckoo people," Grant devised a new way to help them. He taught Nan how to color his lithographs of flowers and fruit. She, in turn, taught Ed, and they received a monthly check for their work. "We saved all we could from the lithographs," Nan said.

This was the era of the crazy landlady who, "If someone was baking a cake, would sneak in and turn off the gas, and they'd have a fallen cake. Sometimes she would sneak in and take their furniture.

"One day she came out in the hall and yelled, 'I'm going to church and all the rest of you can go to hell.' When she left, everyone came out of the rooms and thought of the orneriest thing they could do.

"She hated dogs, so everybody decided to get a dog. On the way to the pound, they found a cocktail party, and when they got there, they were too drunk to know what they came for. Ed and I went home."

After Grant's death, they sold his Iowa City home and were better off than they had ever been in their lives with the money he left them in his will. They attended the opening of the Grant Wood Memorial Exhibition at Chicago's Art Institute and were the luncheon guests of Mrs. Potter Palmer. Even so, Nan made artificial blooms called "American Flowers" to make extra money, and film actress Norma Shearer was one of her customers.

When they moved to a home in Riverside, California, Ed was determined to buy a new car. Nan thought the old car would do a while longer, but she made a bargain with him. If he would agree to stay in the house for a couple of years, he could have the car.

Edward Graham, Grant, and Nan, circa 1940, when Grant worked in Hollywood. Below: 1957 certificate showing Nan's interest in hand-coloring was still alive almost twenty years after she and Ed colored the set of lithographs.

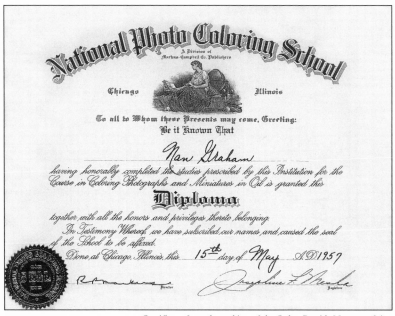

Certificate from the archives of the Cedar Rapids Museum of Art

A stylish blonde Nan Wood Graham met Park Rinard and his new bride, Phyllis, after their marriage in December 1945, at his great-aunt's beach home in Balboa, California.

He had tried to sell the Riverside house before, but she refused to leave it. When he said, "You won't want to stay here alone," she said, "Yes, I will."

The Grahams celebrated their Silver Wedding Anniversary with a trip to Catalina Island in 1949, and six years later Nan sold one of Grant's paintings and told Ed, "I have a surprise for you. We're going to take a trip to Hawaii."

His reply was, "We are not. Hawaii is for kids. We're going to Spain."

Nan was dismayed, and she said, "I didn't want mountains with my high blood pressure. I might have a stroke. The doctor had said I was the type to be smiling and drop dead. At any rate, travel to the awful Spanish mountains would scare me to death."

They argued about it, and Nan asked her doctor if she should risk Spain. At first, he advised her to go. The next day, he reconsidered, suggesting an auto tour of America. Nan said, "Driving in a car made me sick, and the lesser of two evils was going to Europe."

They went, not to Spain, but to Portugal, North Africa, and Italy. Ed contracted food poisoning, something he probably wouldn't have picked up in Hawaii.

Even so, both were eager to embark on a trip around the world, in February 1960, aboard the British liner Iberia. Since it was the liner's first trip to the Orient, they were given the red carpet courtesies.

Editor's note: Text is based on interviews with Nan Wood Graham as taped by the Zugs.

Back to School

by John Fitzpatrick

John Fitzpatrick met Nan Wood Graham while serving as Program Facilitator and Curator for the Fine Arts Collection of the Cedar Rapids School District. In a December 15, 1990 edition of the Cedar Rapids Gazette, *he says of Nan, "She had an artist's temperament not only in her defensive attitude toward people who abused Grant Wood's work, but in her own artistic expression—her glass reverse paintings, her tissue collages, and her creative sewing. When Grant and she went into the country together; he painted, she sewed. She designed and created her own fashions. ...We solicited her opinion on the use of the Cedar Rapids School District's Grant Wood collection."*

The Cedar Rapids Community School District maintains an extensive collection of Grant Wood works. The district collection contains works that Wood created as a student while attending Washington High School (class of 1910), works he did as a faculty member at Jackson and McKinley Junior High Schools, works that were commissioned from him after he left the district, and works that were given to the district by Nan Wood Graham and her brother Frank Wood.

As a student at Washington High School, Wood was involved in the artistic periodical, *The Pulse,* published every six weeks. He was responsible for the design and creation of headings and other art work. Along with his friend, Marvin Cone, he served on the yearbook committee, designing headings, frontispieces, and comics. The two artists created set designs and advertising for school drama productions.

Grant Wood was recognized by Emma Grattan, the Cedar Rapids Schools' art supervisor, as being a very gifted student. Nan tells of Grant's being excused from regular classes to go to Ms. Grattan's office where he could create art.

After painting camouflage for the army during World War I, Wood returned to Cedar Rapids where he taught art for a year in a country school. Through his friendship with Ms. Grattan, he was hired by the Cedar Rapids Community School District to teach art at Jackson Junior High School. Nan became Ms. Grattan's secretary.

Frances Prescott, the principal at Jackson, was hesitant to take Grant onto her staff because of his shy, quiet manner. She felt the students would run roughshod over him. Grant's sense of humor, his genuine concern for students, and his successful pedagogy won over both Miss Prescott and the Jackson students. Miss Prescott became a strong supporter of Grant Wood's artistic work and a life-long friend. Grant and she collaborated in the Community Players—the local community theater. She encouraged the school district to commission his works of art.

One of the first commissioned works was a mural at Harrison School commemorating the Great War (World War I), *Democracy Leading the Way onto Victory*. Figures represented the branches of the armed services in a boat crossing a rough seas. In an early self-portrait, he presents himself as a sailor in the bow of the boat. The work was lost when Harrison School burned to the ground. It was replaced in the new Harrison School with the portable mural, *Transportation*, created by William Henning under the direction of Grant Wood as part of the Public Works of Art Program during the Depression. Wood and Henning met with the students at Harrison to help determine the subject for the mural. This was Wood's practice in the selection of subject and symbolism for district works.

Works were commissioned for Jackson School, *Pine Tree* and *Back of the Pantheon at Sunset*. The latter was commissioned as an unspecific work to help finance his first trip to Europe with Marvin Cone. Later trips to Europe were also financed by patrons who commissioned works. The school district commissioned *Paris 1924—Bridge at Moret* for the dedication of Roosevelt School and *Indian Creek* for the dedication of Franklin School.

When McKinley School was built, Miss Prescott was named principal and took Grant Wood with her. He immediately began decorating the building, and with his students, organized a winter plant care program. Members of the community could bring their large garden plants to the school to be cared for during winter months. More "plants" were modeled by students using found objects in the school shop, *Lilies of the Alley*.

He was commissioned to paint *The Four Seasons Lunettes, Spring, Summer, Autumn,* and *Winter,* to be located over the doors in the library. For his models representing the four ages of man, Grant Wood used McKinley personnel as models: the son of a McKinley teacher, a teacher, a student, and a custodian. He designed and built an arts and crafts style bench in oak and leather for Miss Prescott's office. It was too soft for recalcitrant students and was replaced by a hard, uncomfortable bench he created with manual arts students. On the backrest of the bench was carved the admonition, "The Way of the Transgressor is Hard." His carving skills were further demonstrated in the carving of cork board over a classroom blackboard into a frieze proclaiming "Books Are Magic Doors Through Which One Can Walk Into Innumerable Wonderful Worlds." Students in his classes created a painted frieze, *Imagination Isles*, for the cafeteria. In this project, students integrated the visual image with narrative poetry. Before the frieze was mounted, it was rolled around two drums serving as spindles so that it could be shown scene by scene while the narrative was read. Grant's sense of humor was demonstrated in a papier maché mask titled *Percy, Heavy Thinker*. The mask was worn by the brightest student in class photographs. It was a self-portrait of Grant who, except for art, never made stellar grades.

After he left the school district to devote full time to his career in the arts, Miss Prescott and he provided a unique partnership between the district and the Community Players for use of the McKinley auditorium. The Players could use the auditorium, and Grant would continue to paint backdrops for school productions. The district provided the canvas and paints. One of the backdrops remains on the McKinley stage along with side flats from an earlier Grant Wood backdrop.

After Grant Wood received national recognition for *American Gothic*, he continued to accept memorial commissions from the district. *Young Corn* was commissioned in 1931 as a memorial to a favorite Wilson Junior High School teacher, Linnie Schloeman. Working with the students to determine a subject, they selected a landscape outside Amana. The work represented the nurturing of the young corn, as teachers nurture young students. The students at Wilson School mounted a penny campaign at the height of the Depression to defray the $500 commission. They could raise only $300, which Grant accepted, somewhat unhappily, as full payment. The painting became the subject of Iowa's statehood stamp issued in 1996 to celebrate Iowa's Sesquicentennial. *Arbor Day* was commissioned as a dedication to two teachers who had taught at McKinley School, Catherine Motejl and Rose Waterstradt. Grant again worked with students to determine the subject. Both Motejl and Waterstradt had annually sponsored Arbor Day tree plantings at McKinley.

Grant borrowed the *Arbor Day* painting for an exhibition in Chicago. When he received an offer to sell the painting, he telephoned Miss Prescott for permission to sell the district's painting if he would paint a replacement. Miss Prescott did not have authority to grant permission, but the work was sold. A replacement was never painted. *Arbor Day* has remained in private collections including the

Young Corn *by Grant Wood, 1931*

Memorial to Linnie Schloeman, Woodrow Wilson School

Photograph by John W. Barry

Grant Wood in 1932 stood by his easel holding his completed painting of Arbor Day, *oil on masonite panel, a memorial to Rose Waterstradt and Catherine Motejl, McKinley school. Collection of William I. Koch.*

collection of Hollywood mogul, King Vidor, and is presently in the collection of businessman, William I. Koch. A preparatory drawing for the original painting, *Tree Planting Group*, was finally hung at McKinley School. Wood used this drawing for an edition of lithographs by the same title. Income from the copyrights on *Arbor Day* and *Young Corn* supports the conservation of the entire district art collection.

Grant Wood made a gift of his drawing, *Draft Horse*, to the students of McKinley. He also gave the school the original drawing of *Adolescence*. He said that the awkwardness of puberty that he had seen in his students at McKinley had inspired the work. Many years later, when Miss Prescott retired, she clarified that *Adolescence* had actually been a gift to her, and took the drawing with her. Christian Peterson created a bust of Grant Wood for McKinley School.

The last major commission Grant Wood completed for the district was *Autumn Oaks*, a tribute to Washington High School teacher Elizabeth Cock. Miss Cock was Grant Wood's English teacher. He used the full elegiac symbolism of the autumn season in this work.

During the 1950s, the Cedar Rapids Schools began replacing antiquated facilities. The *Cedar Rapids Gazette* worked with the district to sponsor a contest to name one of the new schools. The winning entry, "Grant Wood," was submitted by Tommy Woodhouse, a student from Buchanan School. Nan was elated to have a school named after Grant Wood. She and her brother Frank came to the dedication bearing gifts. In honor of the Grant Wood School, they presented to the school district seven of the original crayon drawings Grant Wood had done for Madeline Horn's book, *Farm on the Hill*, and one of Grant's lithographs, *March*. The crayon drawings include: *Bold Bug, Early Bird, Escape, Hero Worship, Insect Suicide, Joy Ride,* and *Young Calf*. Nan and Frank also honored Grant Wood's teaching at McKinley School with the gift of five more Grant Wood lithographs: *January, February, March, In the Spring,* and *Family Doctor*.

Additional Wood works have been given to the school district. *Notre Dame*, a painting from Grant Wood's early trip to Paris was given by W.C. Bernsdorf as a memorial to his father-in-law who had been Superintendent of Schools when Grant taught for the district. Mr. Bernsdorf had received the painting as a wedding present from Grant. One of Nan's reverse glass paintings, *Dachshund on Wheels*, was given by Fran Rankin as a memorial to Nan.

Nan remained a loyal supporter of the district collection. During the last years of her life, she worked closely with me as I served as

Program Facilitator for Fine Arts and Curator of the District Collection to develop a collections management policy to protect and safeguard the ownership of the district art collection and to preserve the integrity and value of the collection. Nan felt very strongly that the collection should be shared with a broader audience. To honor Nan's wishes, the Board of Education included the following paragraph in the art collection policy:

"The art collection exists as an important component of the cultural heritage of the District and should be accessible to students and staff. The collection should be promoted for the benefit of the District. As individual works increase in value and prestige, the District assumes a responsibility to make them available to a broader audience beyond Cedar Rapids."

True to Nan's wishes, the District Collection has been made available to a larger audience. *The Four Seasons Lunettes, Bridge at Moret,* and *Autumn Oaks* were part of a major Grant Wood retrospective, "Grant Wood: An American Master Revealed," that traveled to the Joslyn Art Museum, Davenport Museum of Art, and the Worcester Art Museum. *Young Corn* was part of a major scholarly exhibition, "Plain Pictures: Images of the American Prairie," curated by the University of Iowa with additional venues, the Amon Carter Museum of Art and the Joslyn Art Museum.

The District Collections Management Policy allows the Cedar Rapids Community School District to work closely with the Cedar Rapids Museum of Art to afford public access to the collection. Some of the Grant Wood works have become too valuable or too fragile to remain in school buildings. By exhibiting these works through the museum, the district is able to provide public access under the protective care of the professional staff of the museum. In viewing these works with the larger corpus of works owned by the museum, the viewer is able to capture the essence of Grant Wood as he matured from the early formula landscapes to the Impressionist influenced European works to his mature Regionalist style.

Seven of the crayon drawings by Grant Wood for the children's book Farm on the Hill *were given to Grant Wood School, Cedar Rapids, Iowa, by Nan Wood Graham and her brother Frank.*

Originally the drawings were not titled, either in the book or as labels for the drawings. When Grant Wood sent the crayon drawings to the Walker Galleries in New York for exhibition in 1936, the Walker Galleries' brochure titled them all.

Bold Bug, Early Bird, Escape, Hero Worship, Insect Suicide, Joy Ride *and* Young Calf
© *Cedar Rapids, Iowa Community School District*

© Cedar Rapids Community School District , oil on masonite, 30-1/2 x 37 inches

Trees and Hill, *1933*

Faculty Breakfast. June 1923.

Photo from the Cedar Rapids Community School District Archives

Grant Wood is in the front row third from right at a McKinley Junior High School faculty breakfast in 1923.

Grant Wood remembered by his students

Eleanor Cook Thomas, former McKinley Junior High School student remembered:

"Mostly he had the boys for art. They posed and Grant Wood did profiles of each of them and they were simply fantastic. They hung downstairs in his studio and were on heavy brown wrapping paper. There were no names. You just knew them."

In the 1960s Eleanor Cook Thomas introduced transcendental meditation to Iowans in Cedar Rapids after studying in Switzerland.

Jane Carey DeLay said:

"I was a student of Grant's in seventh or eighth grade at Jackson School. I had a terrific crush on him so I do recall those days—1921 or 1922. I remember a couple of projects that he involved us in. One was during the period that everyone was deeply concerned about the starving Armenians. He had us do posters pleading for monetary help for the poor kids."

Jane Carey DeLay successfully lobbied for mental health reform in Iowa in the late 1950s and was listed in Who's Who in America.

Paul Engle, writer and former director of the reknowned University of Iowa International Writing Program, School of Letters, The University of Iowa said in 1977:

"I first saw Grant Wood in eighth grade art class at McKinley Junior High School the year it opened. I arrived late because I had to stay home sick with yellow jaundice the first weeks. We had to letter an elaborate alphabet. Being barely able to sign my name legibly, I turned out letters which obviously caused Grant intense pain when he looked at them. 'Let me show you,' he said, took my pencil and drew a graceful letter S. When we received our work back, my alphabet had on it a note written by Grant: 'This is terrible work, but you can do a fine S. Why?' He was a warm and sympathetic teacher, even to those of us who must surely have looked to him like anti-artists.

"One day he brought a phonograph to class and played a recording of Rimsky-Korsakov's 'Song of India,' while tracing on an abstract painting. He had done the outlines and colors which he alleged represented the musical equivalents. When he became a 'regionalist,' it was amusing to think of his remarks against abstract art. He also told us that a friend of his in Paris had exhibited, to much praise, a painting he had done by setting up an easel in a barn and tying a brush to a donkey's tail and then scratching his hide to make his tail wave back and forth.

"Grant was wonderfully clever with his hands. He had an old sedan car. One winter he built a mechanical arm and hand which he could shove out through a slot when he wanted to make a left turn in the winter so that he need not open the window and let in the cold.

"His humor is sometimes forgotten, but he loved jokes, and knew many—such as one hobo asking another, 'Why do you like to have fantasies about women instead of real women?' The other hobo answered, 'Considering the kind of women I know, I can get a higher type that way.'

"Sudden success also brought almost instant sadness/darkness to Grant. That is another story. He was a gifted, fine, complicated person. As with Robert Frost, his outward cheerful, plain-person image concealed a troubled life."

Children at Grant Wood school in Cedar Rapids dressed as American Gothic *look-a-likes in 1991 when Nan Wood Graham's memorial was held. At left, second row, is the late Carl Smith who gave the Gothic house at Eldon, Iowa, to the State Historical Society of Iowa.*

Grant Wood speaks as teacher and student

"It is of utmost importance to me that any painting should stand the test of abstract design, but a goal of aesthetic purity—if there is such a thing—does not interest me. I want to express something about life that will be intelligible to the average factual-minded person."

And about children and art he said: "It is as natural for children to draw as it is for them to breathe. They are very serious about their earliest efforts. Here is a great test for parental patience. Don't criticize these early gropings. Don't laugh at them. They are important to the children who make them. I was as bashful a child as ever lived. I could not speak a piece at the Sunday school entertainment or sing a song at the school assembly. But I would pour out all of my emotions and longings in a painting, and my mother understood and encouraged me. Everyone should experience this creation."

About his own experiences in school, **Grant Wood** said: "In high school, Mathematics helped me because it is so logical and good taste is largely a matter of logic. Botany and Zoology helped because of the illustrations I had to make for notebooks; classes in English Literature were valuable because writing is so much like painting. Foreign languages! I just couldn't learn one—it was absolutely impossible."

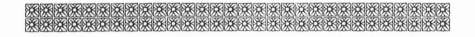

"A work which does not make contact with the public is lost."

"My early work is the result of going around over that very gorgeous territory where I live and not seeing it. I wanted things that looked French. I'd been told that the Middlewest was flat and ugly and I believed it.

"Later, after I realized the material around me was paintable, and started painting out of my own experience, my work had an emotional quality that was totally lacking before. I had to go to France to appreciate Iowa. That was the best way to get perspective."

—*Grant Wood, 1935*

Daughters of Revolution remembered

Joan Liffring-Zug Bourret photo 1960s

Frances Prescott, former principal of McKinley Junior High School who hired Grant Wood to teach art. Her hand was used as a model for the hand holding the tea cup in Daughters of Revolution.

Miss Prescott said in 1951:

"Of course, the picture that caused the most attention and delighted people most was his *Daughters of Revolution*. And when he finished it, he called us and said, 'Wouldn't you like to come over to the studio and see the picture before it goes away?' And so we went over, and I said, 'Grant aren't you sorry to see it go, it's been here so long?' And he said, 'No, I'm not. These old girls have high-hatted me just long enough.'

"When it was on exhibit, a reporter for one of the Pittsburgh papers called him long distance, and asked him if it were true that the head of the D.A.R. in Pittsburgh had posed for the prosperous-looking dowager in the picture. He said it looked enough like her to be a photograph, and Grant assured him that they were imaginary figures. He said, 'Mr. Wood, do you know that they're very much incensed in Pittsburgh?' Grant said no that he didn't. And the reporter said, 'They're so angry, they've hung it behind the door.' And Grant said, 'That's quite all right. I'm painting *Dinner For Threshers* now, and it's 15 feet long, and they won't be able to get it behind a door.'

"Grant said to me one time, 'Whether people approve of my pictures or not isn't what matters. But what does matter is that people should get something out of my pictures, something that would lend in a small measure a certain pattern and clarity to their own experience.'"

Nan Wood Graham had this to say about *Daughters of Revolution:*

"Grant had several reasons for doing *Daughters of Revolution.* The war memorial window he designed for the Coliseum in Cedar Rapids was too large for any stained-glass window people to make in this country. At that time it was to be the largest single stained-glass window in the world and the only place it could be made was in Germany. The D.A.R. objected.

"Besides this, Grant was sick and tired of a little clique of women who had done nothing in this world on their own, put on airs and considered themselves aristocrats and above us common folk, solely because they or their mother belonged to the D.A.R. Grant hated snobbery and said this was supposed to be a free country, and we had no true aristocracy, which is as it should be."

Daughters of Revolution

In 1932, Grant Wood standing by his completed painting Daughters of Revolution, *now in the collection of the Cincinnati Art Museum. On the floor in background is his* Self Portrait, *now in the collection of the Davenport Museum of Art.*

Helen J. Hinrichsen, Davenport, Iowa, artist and friend of Grant Wood, said in 1976:

"One time when I was in Grant Wood's studio at #5 Turner Alley in Cedar Rapids, the postman delivered a letter postmarked Boston, and scrawled across the front of the envelope was 'To the postal authorities of Iowa: Please deliver this to Grant Wood, the artist who painted *Daughters of Revolution.*'"

1975 print based on a 1933 watercolor by the late Helen J. Hinrichsen of Davenport, Iowa, who attended the Stone City Art Colony. Grant Wood is depicted wearing overalls in the center of the print. Hinrichsen is noted for her Davenport Centennial Mural *created in 1936, in the collection of the Davenport Museum of Art. She has exhibited widely throughout the Midwest.*

Stone City Art Colony
Faculty and Students

Group photograph taken at the Stone City Art Colony came from the late Mary Mattern, one of the students. Mary's husband Karl Mattern was an art professor at Drake University. Grant Wood, in overalls, is standing in the back row, second from left.

When Grant Wood's painting of *Stone City* was exhibited at the Iowa State Fair in Des Moines, the artist described an old farmer standing in front of the famous landscape: "The farmer would get up close to the picture, inspect it, and back away shaking his head. I thought if I went up and stood by him, he would say something about the painting. Sure enough, he did. Pretty soon, he shook his head vigorously and said, 'I wouldn't give 35 cents an acre for that land.'"

The rolling hills of Eastern Iowa are particularly beautiful with fields and trees and streams. Grant Wood painted the landscape seen from the top of a hill overlooking the little town and the limestone quarry. The **Grant Wood Festival** is held in Stone City the second Sunday in June.

The Art That Stayed Home

The Cedar Rapids Museum of Art is a major repository of works by Grant Wood, and the most famous painting in the collection is *Woman With Plant(s)*, a portrait of Hattie Weaver Wood, mother of Nan and Grant. People frequently got the title wrong, Nan observed, making it *Woman With Plant*. Mrs. Wood holds one potted variegated snake plant; other plants are in the background.

This portrait was Grant's first painting after his return from Europe, and Mrs. Wood wore the cameo he bought for her there—the same brooch Nan wore in *American Gothic*. It's a wonder that the painting is still in good condition, because he was in a hurry to submit it in a competition at the Art Institute of Chicago. He dried the wet paint over a hot plate, which raised blisters on the canvas. He then carefully pressed the blisters down, and the painting seemed none the worse for it.

Woman With Plant(s) made the show, and Nan said, "We had watched the painting develop stroke by stroke, and to me, it was the most beautiful painting in the world."

Nan came to Cedar Rapids in 1972 for the presentation of the Turner Collection to the museum. John B. Turner II, the son of Grant's patron, David Turner, made the gift because, he said, his family would be scattered about the country, and he considered the collection to be a vital part of the cultural heritage of Cedar Rapids, where it should stay.

David Turner knew nothing about art, Nan said, but after he got to know Grant, he became interested and started to collect. At first, Grant lent him paintings to keep the walls of the mortuary from looking cold and bare, but he was forever taking them back for exhibits. Turner solved the problem by buying everything on the walls.

The Turners gave 84 works by Grant Wood to the Cedar Rapids Museum of Art in 1972. They went on to give 27 more works by Grant Wood and 11 works by Cone.

The Turners gift includes *John B. Turner, Pioneer*, a stern portrait that captures the spirit of one of the founding fathers of Cedar Rapids. It was one of Grant's first works employing the style he developed after studying the paintings of Hans Memling, the fifteenth-century Flemish painter, while in Europe.

The Cedar Rapids Museum of Art had 32 of Grant's works before the Turner gift, and many of those were on loan from the Cedar Rapids Community School District.

Another well-known work is *The Old Shoes,* painted at #5 Turner Alley after Grant and Marvin Cone walked through the mud in a rain storm. The collection also includes paintings Grant did in Europe.

Nan said, "From their earliest high school days, Grant and Marvin were members of the Cedar Rapids Art Association, serving as volunteers for all sorts of duty. They unpacked paintings for exhibition, scraping the paper pasted to the glass with razor blades to keep it from shattering. They slept in the gallery on a cot to guard particularly valuable exhibitions."

The museum has received other gifts of Grant Wood's art, as well. A 1930 painting, *Overmantel Decoration,* which is a Victorian interpretation of the Herbert Stamats family home, is one such gift from Isabel R. Stamats in memory of Herbert S. Stamats. Another gift is *Adoration of the Home,* a mural, which Grant painted for a real estate firm. He disliked his work, and took it back, ostensibly to make some changes, but was sorry it didn't burn in the 1932 fire in his studio.

Nan never saw the new Cedar Rapids Art Museum with its bright, contemporary architectural touches, but she would be pleased with the permanent Grant Wood Gallery that makes the institution a primary repository of her brother's art.

Grant Wood hometown booster

And of his native city, **Grant Wood** said in 1933:

"One of the things of which I'm proudest is the honorary membership which the Cedar Rapids Chamber of Commerce gives me each year."

Grant Wood's unfettered genius

Verne Marshall, Pulitzer Prize Winner for a series of articles exposing sin in Sioux City, Iowa, 320 miles west and editor of the *Cedar Rapids Gazette,* 1931, said:

"I have known Grant Wood for twenty-five years. He was a high school student painting scenery for high school plays when I first became acquainted with him. He had a round, pink face and yellow hair then. He still has. He possessed plenty of talent then. He has much more now. He was modest, whimsical, and wholesome then. He still is. Original, interesting, unafraid, Grant Wood never changes except as his experience improves his skill. And behind all that skill is an intelligence that explains the man's real genius."

Grant Wood's party spirit and attire were often noted by acquaintances. **Catsy Reid Cooper,** whose father was a patron of Grant Wood, said about a Cedar Rapids party held in the 30s:

"The party was given with a nautical theme. Guests had been members of the cast or had worked on the play 'Outward Bound.' Grant surprised us all by coming dressed as a fish. He must have spent hours painting the scales."

Margaret Thoma states in the *Grant Wood Memorial Issue* of *Demcourier,* May 1942:

"To lose sight of Grant Wood's quiet, subtle humor is to misunderstand the man completely. There was little of bitterness or satire in him, much ingenuousness and wit and an infinite capacity to see the funny side of himself. His lithograph *Honorary Degree* means little to the observer unless one recognizes his caricature of himself, pudgy and cherubic, between the two gaunt scholars who make their bestowal."

John B. Turner II recalled in a 1977 letter:

"One of the parts of Grant's life that has never been thoroughly brought out is the excellent iron work which Grant did either by himself or more often with George Wilhelm. I recall that at the time Grant was in Germany doing the stained-glass window for the Memorial Building, that he contacted us and said he felt he had found the solution for the bay window at Turner's Mortuary East.

"He insisted that George design and execute the iron work and Grant did the stained-glass panes. As you know, we have given the Cedar Rapids Art Association a number of Grant's original wrought iron works such as candelabra, door hinges and door pulls, all of which demonstrate the wide variety of Grant's talents.

"I think perhaps it might be well for me to explain the theory upon which Happy and I have made our gifts to the Art Center. We had heard so many stories about how a city, state or country may have acquired the studio or workshop of some famous artist but did not have an adequate number of the artist's work to properly make them available for serious study. This was particularly true of the Impressionist artists of France whose work at the turn of the century was largely ignored in France but seriously collected in the United States, all of which leaves a great gap in French painting. So we decided that the proper way to handle this was an expression of our belief that no paintings should remain in a private collection for over two generations. This met with some disapproval on the part of our sons, but they finally agreed that this would be the only way of creating a focal point where serious artists could come to study his work. I firmly believe that all works of prominence that were done by Grant Wood should be concentrated in Cedar Rapids where he lived and worked."

Joan Liffring-Zug Bourret photo, 1978

John B. Turner II and wife Harriet (Happy) gave the Turner Collection to the Cedar Rapids Museum of Art. The portrait, by Grant Wood, of his grandfather, John B. Turner, Pioneer hangs at the left. Mr. Turner is sitting on Grant Wood's Mourner's Bench at the museum. Wood crafted the bench, while at McKinley Junior High School during the years 1921–1922, for students waiting to see the principal. He carved the words "The Way of the Transgressor is Hard" into the hard oak of the back of the bench designed with three Gothic heads. It is part of the Cedar Rapids Community School District Collection on loan to the museum.

Nan Visits Cedar Rapids Friends

Nan Wood Graham, in white above, met John Zug, left, co-editor of Nan's book My Brother, Grant Wood, *and old friends Winnifred Cone and Gordon Fennell at a 1978 reception in Cedar Rapids. The Cedar Rapids Museum of Art has a gallery named for Mrs. Cone, widow of Grant Wood's lifelong friend and artist colleague, Marvin Cone. Grant Wood painted* Young Gordon, *a portrait of the Fennell's son, which is in the Cedar Rapids Museum of Art Collection. When the portrait of their pre-schooler was first painted, Mr. Fennell said they did not like it, but in later years they loved the portrait. Young Gordon died in his college years.*

After 1970, Nan made several visits to the Grant Wood Art Festival in Stone City, to the Davenport Museum of Art Gallery, and to Cedar Rapids.

Gordon Fennell, distributor of Cedar Rapids food products worldwide and friend of Grant Wood, said in 1977:

"I was active with the Community Players. At that time, although Grant could ill afford it, he gave unstintingly of his advice and time to the Community Players, and without compensation prepared many of the stage paintings and decorations. His helpfulness and advice could not be measured by money."

Back Where They Belong

The Grant Wood collection that his sister Nan sold to the Davenport Municipal Art Gallery included a number of original paintings, drawings, sketches and lithographs. The most important work was his self-portrait painted in 1932.

Other paintings were *Quivering Aspen*, an oil sketch on wood which was Nan's seventeenth birthday present from her brother, and *Iowa Cornfield* painted in 1941, the last year of his life.

Oil sketches of *Truck Garden Moret, Paris, Stone City, Fall Plowing, Chapel Chancelade*, and his final oil study, *Iowa Landscape* (done in 1941) were part of the purchase. Also there were large charcoal drawings illustrating the history of writing, sketch books of ideas for the *Memorial Window* in Cedar Rapids, thirteen original lithographs and pencil sketches for "The Wolf and the Lamb," an unpublished poem about Hitler and Chamberlain.

A watercolor he painted in 1907, *Currants*, was included, and so was a tiny watercolor titled *Country Church*, and the master set of lithographs of tame and wild flowers, fruits and vegetables that the artist tinted himself. He later brought Nan back from California to teach her how to tint the prints, and she and her husband supplemented their income in that way for a number of years.

Elizabeth Rochow was director of Davenport Municipal Art Gallery when the purchase was made, and she was overjoyed to take possession of some of the works that had been exhibited at the museum's 1957 retrospective, "Grant Wood and the American Scene." Nan attended the opening of that exhibit, sitting up on a train all night to get to Davenport. Her warm reception there had a lot to do with the disposition of the collection.

Mrs. Rochow's successor, L. G. Hoffman, later said, "The unique Grant Wood collection, developed over the years from a modest beginning of several original lithographs, offers the visitor an in-depth glimpse of Grant Wood.

"Perhaps the most astonishing statements of the collection are reflected in his preliminary oil studies. Grant Wood compromised between abstraction and reality. Until he was satisfied with the semi-abstract composition and design of his idea, he would not begin the meticulous detail of his precise rendering style. The oil studies can be viewed with initial aesthetic form as Grant Wood visualized.

"The total picture of the artist must be sought in his homeland, his alpha and omega. Davenport Municipal Art Gallery takes pride in sharing its salute to Iowa's native son."

The gallery's name changed to the Davenport Museum of Art in 1987, and in 1996 it mounted a traveling exhibit of Wood's art, "Grant Wood: An American Master Revealed," which drew record crowds in Davenport, Iowa; Omaha, Nebraska, and Worcester, Massachusetts.

William Steve Bradley, director of the Davenport Museum of Art, along with the directors at the other sites, noted the tendency to overlook the complexities of Wood's personality and artistic vision because of the popularization of his art. "The exhibit and catalog demonstrate that Wood's artistic vision did not develop in a midwestern vacuum but instead drew heavily on sources ranging from Georges Seurat to Neue Sachlichkeit to Arts and Crafts design principles."

The museum recruited a team of conservators to make the first systematic, technical examination of Grant Wood's paintings, giving a complete profile of his materials and techniques. For instance, X-radiographs showed the underlying design of the paintings, finding them nearly identical to the charcoal sketches in many cases.

The entire exhibit was inspired by the plein-air oil studies Wood created in Europe in the 1920s, the oil sketches Nan sold to the museum. Brady Roberts, the curator who organized the exhibit, also recognized similarities between Grant Wood and Georges Seurat, the French pointillist, as well as between the Iowan and Otto Dix, the Munich artist who layered his works like the old masters. Roberts passed through the lower gallery where Wood's art was displayed frequently, and one day he had a revelation about Wood's painting—a synthesis of styles: Northern Gothic, early Italian Renaissance, Neo-Impressionism and Neue Sachlichkeit (modern German). The exhibit with an X-ray vision of Wood's vision followed.

Through the years the Davenport Museum of Art has been proud of the Wood collection and has added to it the oil painting, *Spotted Man*, and *The Booster*, a large charcoal, pencil and chalk drawing.

Even though the images Grant Wood created have circled the globe repeatedly, many of them have taken root in the soil where he planted them—the Midwest in general and Iowa in particular. Nan wanted to find a good home for the works in her possession, and it seems that she did. Iowa appreciates its native son and his art.

The whereabouts of other works by Grant Wood

Paintings that were part of Nan Wood Graham's life for awhile can be found in museums and private collections all over America. At the time of her death in December 1990, the ownership of most had stabilized, and she knew where Grant's works were displayed.

She was always proud when someone famous purchased her brother's art, for instance, when Edward G. Robinson bought *Daughters of Revolution* for $2,000 in the late 1930s. She was equally pleased when Stavros Niarchos, the Greek shipping magnate, bought it for $67,000 in 1958. Presently, the painting is owned by the Cincinnati Museum of Art.

The Art Institute of Chicago has owned *American Gothic* since 1930 and is loathe to lend it to other institutions. *Portrait of Nan*, which was bought for the Encyclopedia Britannica Collection, now is on loan to the Elvehjem Museum of Art, University of Wisconsin, Madison, from the collection of William Benton, a Britannica executive. *Midnight Ride of Paul Revere* is in the collection of the Metropolitan Museum of Art, New York City; *Haying* is in the National Gallery of Art, Washington; *Dinner for Threshers* is in the Fine Arts Museum of San Franciso; *Fall Plowing* is in the John Deere Art Collection, Moline, Illinois, and *Parson Weems' Fable* is owned by the Amon Carter Museum, Fort Worth, Texas.

While the Davenport and Cedar Rapids museums own the bulk of Grant Wood's output, the Carnegie-Stout Free Public Library in Dubuque has *Victorian Survival* and *Appraisal*. The University of Iowa Museum has *Plaid Sweater*, and the study for *The Birthplace of Herbert Hoover*, and the oil painting of the Hoover home is owned jointly by the Des Moines Art Center and the Minneapolis Institute of Arts.

Stone City can be found in the Joslyn Art Museum, Omaha; *Arnold Comes of Age* is in the Sheldon Memorial Art Gallery, University of Nebraska, Lincoln, and Cole Porter gave *Death on the Ridge Road* to Williams College Museum of Art.

Two murals, *Breaking the Prairie Sod* and *When Tillage Begins, Other Arts Follow*, were commissioned by Iowa State University, Ames, and are found in the Parks Library.

Coe College, Cedar Rapids, is the home of a collection of oil on canvas works: *Boy Milking Cow, Farmer's Wife, Farm Landscape, Basket of Fruit, Farmer's Son, Farmer's Daughter*, and *Farmer with Pigs*.

The lithographs *Honorary Degree, Fertility, Wild Flowers, Vegetables, Shrine Quartet,* and *The Perfectionist* are in the collection of the Fine Arts Museum of San Francisco's Achenback Foundation for Graphic Arts.

Many more studies, drawings and lithographs are in museum collections across the land, and the works in private collections are mainly floral still lifes and some landscapes from Wood's Frenchified period in the mid-1920s. Even these works are finding their way, gradually, to museum collections.

Memorable quotes

Ludwig Mies van der Rohe, famous architect, was a guest with Grant Wood at a ranch in Wyoming and remembered:

"But on a ranch, one must do something, so Grant Wood said, '**I will milk a cow.**' And every morning for three days he milked her. Then he tired of the cow, so for two mornings he did nothing. The third morning a noise came at his bedroom window and there was the cow. 'See?' Grant said, 'Now she comes to me.'"

(1937)

Two years later Grant said, "**Suddenly I became aware that my very best ideas of art had come to me while milking a cow in Iowa.**"

(1939)

Grant would most likely would have been a farmer if he hadn't been an artist, according to Nan Wood Graham, he stated:

"I'm just a simple middle western farmer-painter, and painting is more work than people realize. I think I'm doing well to do two pictures a year that satisfy me after spending long and tedious work in research and sketching."

Grant Wood remembered

For the catalog of an exhibition, Lakeside Press Galleries, Chicago, 1936, **Arnold Pyle** and **Park Rinard** wrote:

"His people were Quakers and he remembers his father returning an unread copy of *Grimm's Fairy Tales* to a neighbor, thanking him but saying, 'We Quakers can only read true things.' The boy's first drawing was of his favorite Plymouth Rock hen sitting on an impossible number of eggs. 'The only drawing materials I could get,' he says, 'were large sheets of cheap, white cardboard that were enclosed in the wooden boxes of huge square crackers that Father bought in Anamosa. My first studio was underneath the oval dining room table which was covered with a red checkered cloth. The cloth hung with nice arched openings on both sides.' Such things as the tangy smell of buffalo robes remembered from winter sleigh rides, the soft patter of summer rain on the low farmhouse roof, and particularly the velvet thrill of the cool earth on his bare feet as he walked across the plowed field to school were later to vitalize his portrayals of the scenes and people he knew."

William J. Henderson, trustee Davenport Municipal Art Gallery, said in 1977:

"During the winter between the Stone City sessions of 1932 and 1933, the Tri-City Arts League of Davenport held a Mardi Gras Gala. Club members tried to top each other with their costumes. The high point of the evening was when Grant Wood made his entrance as a lion tamer decked out in leotard and sandals laced to his knees. He had driven over from Cedar Rapids."

Grant Wood Slept Here

The Davenport Museum of Art's Grant Wood Collection, purchased from Nan Wood Graham for $30,000 late in 1964, numbers 381 art works and personal possessions of the artist, including his Hollywood bed with a rich green padded headboard and bolsters.

Wood's self-portrait alone was worth the price, but the purchase included other works of art and a generous slice of his life. Everything from his silver baby cup to the American flag that covered his coffin is in the collection, and the Wood family heritage is preserved in his mother's mourning veil, his father's glasses, daguerreotypes of parents and ancestors, silver spoons, and ironstone tableware.

The artist's easel and palette are in the collection as is the red flannel undershirt he procured with great difficulty for a painting he never made and the cameo brooch, immortalized in *American Gothic,* which Wood bought for his mother in Europe.

After Wood's death in 1942, his sister moved these possessions to California, hoping to create there a replica of his house at 1142 Court Street, Iowa City. A brick mansion of the Civil War era was impossible to achieve in wartime California, but Nan found a place for her brother's art and personal effects in a house with a contemporary exterior.

Nan was received warmly at a retrospective of Wood's work at the Davenport Municipal Art Gallery in 1957, and the possibility of a Grant Wood Corner was discussed. She prepared herself to give up the precious things her brother had willed to her.

"It was my intention never to part with Grant's things, especially his self-portrait," she said, "but time changes everything. If I let Grant's things go now, I will have the satisfaction of knowing what has become of them and knowing they are in the right place."

Administrators of the University of Iowa Art Museum thought it was the right place, and so did the Cedar Rapids Museum of Art. When the Davenport Municipal Art Gallery paid $30,000 for the collection, a Cedar Rapids editorial noted: "Davenport is in the appropriate state, at least, for local pride indulgence," concluding that the editorial in a scrapbook reads: "Sour grapes."

Until the early 1990s, Grant Wood's parlor and bedroom were re-created at the Davenport Museum of Art with his Victorian sofa, shelves of his books, tier tables which he made from Victorian picture frames, lamps, decorative glass pieces, the padded Hollywood bed, and the lounge chair and ottoman he designed with a life-sized cut-out of the artist standing beside it.

That space is now an interactive art area for children, but Grant Wood's domestic treasures were displayed in the 1996 exhibit, "Grant Wood: An American Master Revealed."

Reproductions of the black-and-white lithographs were sold by Armstrong's Department Store. Grant Wood worked with the Robert Armstrongs to design many of the details to show early pioneer architecture in their stone home in Cedar Rapids. The cardboard cut-out of Grant is standing behind one of the lounge chairs he designed. All are in the collection of the Davenport Museum of Art.

A Forty-Year Correspondence

Grant's friends became Nan's friends, and Ed Green, editor of the *Iowa City Press Citizen* in the 40s, saved the letters she wrote to him from 1947 to 1987. He was her confidant, and she told him everything that was on her mind.

In June 1947 she offered to sell him Grant's "wrapping paper drawing" of the birthplace of Herbert Hoover for $100, saying, "Don't take it unless you want it." He took it, and it is now in the collection of the University of Iowa Museum, valued at more than $300,000.

She also shared some skeletons in the family closet, such as "Grandfather Wood was mean to his boy," and "Uncle Clarence beat a calf with a shovel and beat a horse with a two-by-four." She noted that Grant didn't like to visit with the Woods because "Aunt Sallie was a terrible cook and so nearsighted that you never knew what you might find in your food."

The letters reveal that Aunt Sallie lengthened all of Nan's dresses when she came to visit because "Uncle Clarence wouldn't want me going around in dresses that looked like bathing suits." Aunt Sallie's wardrobe was eccentric—long underwear, long bloomers, a short-sleeve chemise, two ruffled underskirts, one dress on top of another.

Nan bragged about the vocabulary of her parakeet—seventy-seven words—and kept Ed Green informed of her frequent address changes. In 1959, she wrote, "It's just another house, but we got it on a big buy." The postmarks changed frequently: Glendora, Upland, Arlington, and finally Riverside.

She told Green about the Davenport Municipal Art Gallery buying Grant's last sketch, the study for *Iowa Cornfield,* because Ed was with Grant when he did it.

A 1960 Christmas card shows Nan and her husband at the Great Pyramids of Giza, a stop on their round-the-world tour, and the next year she shared the dread news of Ed Graham's cancer.

In 1963, she talked about her own glaucoma, and two years later reported "a miserable trip to Florida and the Bahamas. Both of us were sick with colds."

One can only guess at the reason for her letter of May 12, 1966, saying, "Please, don't worry about us thinking you are cashing in on your friendship with Grant. We all know that you lean over backwards not to. I suppose people say that about me, but I don't care.

I'm proud of having Grant for a brother and having posed for *American Gothic*, and I don't care who knows it or what they say. You should feel that way too, Ed, because you really were close to Grant and one of his best friends."

She shared her joys saying, "I never dreamed that there would be a wax model of me during my lifetime." She also shared her sorrow, writing, "The news is very bad—cancer of the bone. He (Ed Graham) still thinks it is arthritis, so be very guarded in what you say."

A letter written in August 1967, after Ed's death, says, "I miss Ed so. It isn't too bad in the daytime when I am busy, but the evenings are so lonesome, as I am always alone."

Through the years, she chronicles her efforts to get a book about Grant published and the problem of granting rights to his works. She hoped Park Rinard would do the book, but, she said, "After twenty-five years, he will never write it, as much as he would love to."

She sent an article about Sara, Grant's ex-wife, to Ed Green in 1969, saying, "Glad she didn't say anything about Grant. Kind of pitiful, isn't it? Living in a shack and on social security." The same letter said, "So many people wanted to write Grant's autobiography. Seven so far, and none suitable."

In June 1969, she told Ed, "Scribners found a writer, but he was such a big-shot that he didn't want my name on the book and wanted to dig out his own material from the source. I held out on it." She continued to work on the manuscript herself.

Later that month she wrote, "Money from selling the collection to Davenport is a godsend to me now, for, no doubt, I would have had to go to work at my age."

She shared the details of her appearance on "To Tell The Truth" in 1970, writing, "Kitty Carlyle is the only one who guessed me." She also tried to persuade Green to collaborate on her book about Grant.

Describing the earthquake of March 1971, she wrote, "Everything hopped up-and-down like popcorn." A month later she told of "a big party in a swell Beverly Hills home. Before it ended, four fully-clothed men and one woman were in the pool."

In August of that year, she told Ed about her heart attack.

A letter written March 15, 1974, says, "Did I tell you I am fed up on what MacKinlay Kantor has to say about Grant?" Later, in 1977, MacKinlay Kantor wrote: "It is grotesque to record that he died in 1942, two hours short of his fifty-first birthday. He deserved better than that, and so did the wide generations who admired and respected Grant Wood."

She passed along a letter from William Shirer written in January 1977 saying, "One day shortly after the war, Grant's wife, or divorced wife, barged in on me at my office at CBS. I can't remember much about it except she whined a lot and seemed bitter about Grant's friends in Cedar Rapids and Iowa City whom, as I recall, she blamed for the breakup. She was seeking a career in New York."

In May of that year, Nan wrote, "Park said, 'Ed Green wears well.' Not everybody does."

She shared the sad news that Scribners had rejected her manuscript in April 1981, and in October 1982 she wrote, "If only I hadn't sold my portrait or Grant's portrait I wouldn't have to worry today whether I am going to have enough money to last me out."

Her letter to Ed in February 1986 is impossible to read because of her failing eyesight, and an interpretation by Pauline Cogswell was enclosed. She wrote even more illegibly in May 1987, and her dictated Christmas message of that year ended the correspondence. She said, "I'm in a nursing home. Pauline is taking care of my affairs. This is my second year of total darkness. It was hard to take at first, but now I'm used to it. I guess you know that recently Grant's painting, *Arbor Day,* sold for $1,375,000."

Ed Green was, indeed, a friend who wore well. He saved Nan's letters for the rest of his life, and his niece Jeannine Enwright contributed them and a number of *American Gothic* parodies and clippings about Grant to the Davenport Museum of Art in 1998. The letters are a candid record of Nan Wood Graham's concerns for forty years, written to a man she trusted because Grant Wood valued his friendship.

Grant's Final Painting: *Spring In Town*

Sketching a house in Northeast Iowa City

Sketching in his own backyard

Grant Wood autographs a sketch to his good friend, Ed Green, an editor of the Iowa City Press Citizen. *At his right is the painting* Spring In Town. *In 1941, Grant worked at his Kare No More Studio in Clear Lake, Iowa.*

Nan Wood Graham

by James P. Hayes

Nan visited Jim Hayes, right, in his home, once the residence of Grant Wood in Iowa City, Iowa. While the 1978 television is new, the bookcases remain the same as when Grant Wood lived there. Others shown are from left: Edwin B. Green, Bernie Asmundsen, and Nan Wood Graham.

My recollection is of meeting Nan first in either 1976 or 1977, when she made a visit to my home at 1142 East Court Street. This was her first visit since the sale of the house to Dr. Pauline Moore.

Nan had been Executor of Grant Wood's estate following his death in February 1942. At that time, she stayed in Iowa City long enough after his funeral to conclude the sale and then hurried back to her husband in California.

On her visit to Iowa City in the late 70s, Ed Green, a friend of Grant and Nan, accompanied Nan to my house. I had a dinner for six or eight people, and remember Nan as being charming and funny. She was thrilled to see the house and walk through the rooms. She remembered *Life* magazine's photographers setting up their equipment on the dining room table, which Grant had built, and shooting pictures of Grant in the living room.

Nan recalled Grant's designing the twelve dining room chairs, which were then made in Amana. She said the acorn design on the chairs was meant to reflect the same design as on the finials of the fence and the cornice of the house, and to commemorate the builder of the house, Nicholas Oakes—originally spelled Oaks.

We stopped in the east bedroom upstairs, which had been Park Rinard's room when he served as Grant's secretary. I had laid out, on the bed, pictures from an artist's portfolio which Nan had left in the house for Dr. Moore and which Dr. Moore left for me. The portfolio had belonged to Grant. Nan carefully inspected the array of water colors, oils, charcoals and pencil drawings. She thought they were the work of Grant's students. Suddenly she snatched one of the pictures from the pile. It was a series of pencil sketches or drawings on brown wrapping paper, all folded into a neat rectangular form with the images on the top side. She held the drawing up and said, "Jim, this is very valuable. This is Grant's work. I'm sure it's never been seen before. You must frame this and keep this." I did both, and the picture hangs in the dining room.

After our stroll around the house, Ed Green, Nan, and I had our picture taken together on the sofa in front of the old rosewood square piano which had been in the house when Grant lived there. Grant had purchased it for his wife, Sara. Nan also told me how she and Grant and her husband had hand colored the lithographs, *Wild Flowers, Tame Flowers, Fruits,* and *Vegetables* in the kitchen at a long, black table. She said that Associated American Artists had commissioned Grant to do these pictures, and he used the money to buy canvas and oil for his bigger pieces.

Nan talked of all the bright red paint Grant had used in the kitchen which could be found in the interior of cupboards and on the ceilings of the kitchen and the pantry. Dr. Moore had covered the red ceiling in the kitchen with a dropped ceiling in the 1950s, but the pantry still had the red paint on oilcloth over plaster. Nan looked up at it and said, "You can tell people you have an original Grant Wood oil painting," and I have ever since.

I had always found particularly interesting and beautiful a sculptured sort of "scooped out" limestone piece in the image of a clam which had been placed by Dr. Moore under an outside faucet on the east side of the house. The lower half of the block of stone had broken away due to the freezing and thawing process, and I had brought the piece into the screened porch off the dining room. Nan was so surprised and pleased to see this object. She said, "Grant designed a reflecting pool for the lower back yard, and this pool was to be rimmed with clam shells sculptured out of blocks of limestone. He finished only one before he died. This is it."

In 1993 when I was remodeling the kitchen and we were taking the walls down to the brick and the ceiling up to the original ceiling, we found, first, the famous Grant Wood red ceiling in the kitchen. Then as we removed wainscoting from the plastered walls, beside the doorway to the dining room, we found a perfectly scaled pencil drawing of the reflecting pool which Nan had described during her visit. Because the plaster was so unstable, we were unable to salvage that portion of the wall, but I took photos of the drawing and had a friend hold the one stone sculpted piece next to the drawing in a photo to show what Grant Wood had intended.

Nan returned to visit 1142 one more time before her death, and she and Ed Green had their picture taken next to the picket fence in front of the house.

Joan Liffring-Zug Bourret photo, 1978

Interior Views of Grant Wood's Home
1934–1942

An old rosewood piano emphasized the Early American furnishings of the living room (top). The wallpaper was an imported French Victorian rose design. Grant Wood designed his large dining room table, using cast-iron supports from old store counters as legs. An open cupboard contained a large flint glass collection.

Grant Wood's bedroom contained an antique pedestal table, a whatnot for books, and a wall alcove for personal photos. The drapes were fringed white corduroy, and wallpaper was a green and white ivy design.

The kitchen with a radio and an antique castor set on the table where many meals were taken.

Grant Wood, standing, wearing a fake mustache, and regional artist Thomas Hart Benton, with a fake beard, are ready for a meeting of the Society of Prevention of Cruelty to After Dinner Speakers. Many famous people visited Grant, including Carl Sandburg, during the 1930s and early 40s.

Grant Wood as teacher and mentor

Professor Willis Guthrie, Carroll College, Waukesha, Wisconsin, recalled in 1977:

"In order to enlarge my stock of painting supplies, Wood provided work around his home in Iowa City, which gave me some assistance in supporting myself as a student. I alternated between the role of hired hand and guest—wearing the same overalls in both functions. I would often be called from yard work to join Wood and his guests—artists and writers—and I would eat and laugh as heartily as the rest. His cook and housekeeper was an Amish girl with a real talent for serving wonderful dinners. The table was set with antique ironstone china from a loaded sideboard.

"Practicality was important to Wood. He wore overalls when he painted or worked in the garden. His knowledge of garden craft was good, and he was very concerned about how his plants related to the warm colors of the fine old sand brick house. The wall around his yard was neatly laid stone surmounted by a durable wooden picket fence. A series of main support posts carried iron acorns about six inches high which he had designed himself. The gate latch, which was first a barn door latch, proved to be unsatisfactory, so he designed a latch with a vertical arm ending with a knob which could be tripped with an elbow as you entered with an armload of groceries or bundles. I think I mention this latch only because draftsmanship of the working plan prepared the carpenter and handyman, Mr. Kuhn. It was done on brown wrapping paper with the same devotion he (Wood) had given the *Main Street* characters.

"His classes were taught with step-by-step procedures for producing a rational painting which denied chance or impulse. He was Mondrian not a DeKooning. He had a fine and subtle sense of humor enjoyed by his students as well as his friends, including Carl Sandburg, Lawrence Tibbett, and Eric Knight.

"He shared many of his experiences about the background of his works and the conditions under which they were done. He gave very freely of his time to students..."

John Barry photograph, 1932–1933

John Steuart Curry, left, and Grant Wood share a happy moment at the Stone City Art Colony in 1932–1933. Curry was a Regionalist painter from Kansas.

John Steuart Curry, artist and friend of Grant Wood, said in the May, 1942 Memorial Issue of *Demcourier:*

"...Grant inspired and taught the young painters...that in their own environment there is a wealth of material to interpret. It was once nearly impossible for an American artist to receive recognition without going to Europe to paint. ...Grant, through his own work of teaching and lecturing, helped to change that. ...And because of his sincerity, his earnest belief in this philosophy of doing the thing you understand and love best, he has received world-wide acclaim. ...

"Contrary to many a layman critic, Grant's painting is not realism, nor is it realistic. He formalized and characterized his subjects. That was his special talent, his unique ability. He could make one face in a picture represent and interpret the lives and souls of a whole group of people."

America's Enduring Symbol

Joan Liffring-Zug Bourret photo, 1975

Descendants of Dr. Byron McKeeby, Grant's dentist who posed for American Gothic, stand by a print of the painting at Fred Bjornson's insurance company in the 1970s. They are the late Gerald McKeeby and his daughter Gerri Repass of Cedar Rapids.

Nan Wood Graham in a July 9, 1995 interview recalled that her brother helped and encouraged young artists. "He gave free criticism and when he was a professor at the University of Iowa, he had the use of their old surgical amphitheatre. Paintings were shown there. …Painters, young and old, from all over came to have free critiques."

From left: Mrs. Willis Mercer, Nan, and Mrs. A. W. Bennett, Iowa City Public Library, 1978 reception for Nan Wood Graham. On the wall in the background is a print of the Midnight Ride of Paul Revere.

Mrs. A. W. Bennett, widow of Grant Wood's physician who posed for *Family Doctor,* said in 1977:

"They had a tremendous respect for each other and each other's work. But they did poke fun at each other. Once my husband was kidding him about the rabbit tracks in the *January* drawing, and he asked him if he had ever seen a rabbit jump in a straight line like that. Grant replied that if he should ever want to paint a picture exactly as it was, he would just take a photograph."

Nan Wood Graham, when asked if she thought Grant Wood died feeling that he might have done more..., replied:

"He put it out of his mind that he wasn't going to live and made plans for the future, and he said he worked best in the studio where he worked and slept and ate under the same roof, and that he was going to paint a portrait of our father to match up with the *Woman with Plant(s)*. He had all kinds of plans made, but, of course, it was too late. But the plans were to keep his mind off what was to come."

Letters Reveal Nan's
Careful Watch over Grant's Legacy

Curt and Norma Hames of Cedar Rapids, Iowa, have graciously provided correspondence between Nan Wood Graham and editors of *The Saturday Evening Post* in 1965, concerning a letter from Nan which was published in the magazine. Norma Hames purchased the letters from the estate of Mrs. Arnold Pyle.

Nan to Mr. Emerson of *The Saturday Evening Post*:
October 27, 1965

Dear Mr. Emerson:

I have just finished reading the very fine article about Mr. Thomas Benton, by Robert Wernick, in your Oct. 23rd issue.

As I am the sister of the late Grant Wood, I was much interested and concerned about Mr. Benton saying Grant had died in despair.

Also, in an article in 1951, in *The Saturday Review of Literature*, Mr. Benton said, "In the end, what with worry over weighty debts and artistic self-doubts, Wood came to the strange idea of changing his identity. Grant Wood was man of many curious and illusory fancies. When I went to see him in 1942, as he lay dying of liver cancer* in an Iowa hospital, he told me when he got well he was going to change his name, go where nobody knew him and start all over again with a new style of painting. This was very uncanny because I'm sure he knew quite well he would never come out of the hospital alive. It was as if he wanted to destroy what was in him and become an empty soul before he went out into the emptiness of death."

Before going any further, may I say that Mr. Benton was a true and sincere, and a loyal friend to Grant, and Grant in turn thought the world of him. Mr. Benton had every reason to believe that Grant died in despair, and I feel that I have done both Grant and Mr. Benton a great injustice in not writing this letter of explanation long, long, ago.

*Correction: Grant Wood died of pancreatic cancer.

After Grant had been told that he had cancer, and that there was no hope, Grant asked to be left alone for a while in order to adjust to the idea. Later, he told his private secretary and friend Park Rinard that he was going to shut it out of his mind (a power which Grant seemed to have) and said he was going to go on just as he had before his illness, making plans for the future. This was Grant's way of sparing his loved ones as much as possible, and he had so lived that he had no fear of meeting his maker.

I had arrived from California the next day. As I entered the hospital, Grant had the most wonderful and serene smile on his face. I cried, "Oh, Grant they shouldn't have told you!" And, Grant replied, "I should know." These were the only words ever spoken to me of his impending death, or to anyone else, to my knowledge, unless it was his minister or his doctors. During the days that followed, Grant was under sedation, morphine alternated with snake venom. All his life Grant had many ideas and plans. Too many for any one man to ever carry out. Now each day there was a new plan, and the plan was helped along by the drugs.

Once he told me that he was going to have his house put up for sale. He was going to buy a house in Palm Springs, and he wanted my husband and I to live with him. He told me to be on the lookout for an Oriental houseboy.

When Grant told Mr. Benton that when he got well he was going to change his name and start all over again, it was just another of many plans.

One of Grant's last plans was to come home and paint. He said to me, "things worked out best for me in the studio (in Cedar Rapids) when I lived, ate, slept and worked all under one roof and Mom did the cooking." He went on to say, "Have my room made ready and my easel set up. I'm coming home to paint. In the year ahead, I'm going to do the best work of my life. My first painting will be a portrait of our father. It will be a companion piece to *Woman With Plant(s)* (our mother).

Each plan was so realistic, that it was hard to believe Grant knew he would never get well. If he had not spoken those few words to me when I first arrived home, I would have thought he didn't know.

The afternoon before Grant lapsed into a comma, a few of his close friends and I gathered at his bedside to drink a last t ast to him, as we had been told the end was near. That night Grant lapsed into a coma from which he never awoke.

In spite of his being troubled by heavy sniping of small, jealous people, Grant had everything going for him when he died. He and his colleagues, John Curry and Thomas Benton, were the Big Three of the art world. Grant's paintings were in great demand, some selling even before they were completed, and they commanded big prices.

He had almost climbed out of debt, and the chaos of his marriage, and had regained his zest for life. He had reached the very peak. I would say that Grant went out in a blaze of glory, rather than the depths of despair. I am enclosing a copy of this letter. Would you be so kind to forward it on to Mr. Benton as I do not know his address.

I feel this letter will be of comfort to him and to other of Grant's true friends to know that Grant did not die in despair.

Sincerely,
[signed Nan Wood Graham]
(The woman in *American Gothic*)

Barbara J. Posen (an editor of *The Saturday Evening Post*) replied to Nan:

November 5, 1965

We are very grateful to have read the moving account of your brother's final days. May we share your memories with those who have long loved and respected the work of Grant Wood? With your consent, we shall publish the story on our Letters page.

Thank you for your thoughtful consideration of this request.

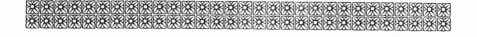

Acknowledging Ms. Posen's interest in her letter, Nan wrote:

Nov. 9, 1965

Thank you so much for your kind letter in regard to my brother Grant Wood.

I am very pleased to give you permission to publish my former letter. There have been so many, many things written about Grant that were not true, that I welcome this opportunity to publicly set, at least one, straight.

In the case of Thomas Benton, it was purely a misunderstanding for he loved and honored Grant. But that terrible book, supposedly about Grant by Darrell Garwood, is another story. It is full of lies and half-truths worse than lies. It was meant to belittle Grant and his achievements, and was a triumph to Grant's enemies.

The worst part of it is, this book is now quoted as the bible on Grant, as the true story of his life has never been written, although it was contracted for long before his death.

It is my fond hope that someday, during my lifetime, the true story of Grant will be written.

This letter is of course, confidential.

Thanking you many times, and with all best wishes, I am
Sincerely,
[signed Nan Wood Graham]

Editor's note: Nan's biography *My Brother, Grant Wood,* written with Julie Jensen McDonald and John Zug, was published by the State Historical Society of Iowa in 1993.

Following publication of her letter, Nan wrote:

Jan. 9, 1966

Dear Miss Posen:

I want to thank you and *The Saturday Evening Post* for publishing my letter about my brother, the late Grant Wood, and for the opportunity to let the world know the truth.

I am so happy over the results. Letters have come from many places concerning it. The *Cedar Rapids Gazette* had quite an article about it, and I received a letter from Edwin B. Green, Editor of the *Iowa City Press Citizen* in which he said: "I enjoyed your letter in *The Saturday Evening Post* so much and was so glad you straightened out the record; as all of us know, Grant did not die in despair. I've had many, many people call my attention to your letter. More power to you!"

But the very best letter of all was the one you published in your Jan. 15th issue—the letter by Miss? Mary C. Drew. I was so touched that a complete stranger to me would take the time at this busy, busy season to write such a wonderful letter.

Thank you for publishing her letter also.

I wonder if I could bother you to forward the enclosed letter of thanks to her, as I do not know her complete address.

Thank you for everything, I am
> Sincerely,
> [signed Nan Wood Graham]

Response from Barbara J. Posen:

January 14, 1966

Dear Mrs. Graham:

We're very pleased to hear about the results of our publication of your letter. But we're the ones who are grateful for having had the opportunity to share your comments with our readers.

We'll certainly forward your thanks on to Mary C. Drew.

Our very warmest wishes.
> Sincerely,
> Barbara J. Posen

Politically correct in the 1980s?

An article by **Robert Hullihan** in the *Des Moines Sunday Register*, October 2, 1983, begins:

"Although one of the world's most famous works of art was painted by an Iowan in Iowa, the Iowa Development Commission would just as soon it had never happened. ..."

The commission's "State of Minds" campaign was an effort to attract silicon chip variety industry to Iowa. Hullihan says, "The problem is that the humorless man with the pitchfork and the suspicious woman beside him (*American Gothic*) do not look like 'high-tech types.' They stand before their Gothic window as though barring the way to the electronic future.

"The commission's slick ads and word play seem to shrivel up under the gaze of the righteous pair. ..."

The commission acknowledged, however, that Grant Wood is mentioned in several of the state's brochures.

"It's famous, but do we want it in the middle of downtown?"

Alexandra Tomes, Executive Director, Cedar Rapids-Marion Arts Council, said January 9, 1984:

"I like the concept of a piece of public art—but I would like to see a piece of art that hasn't had so many unfortunate renderings... I don't think I want to see it as the symbol of the city I live in."

Ms. Tomes emphasized that she was speaking for herself and not the entire Arts Council. The idea of a downtown plaza with a life-size scene from Grant Wood's immortal painting, *American Gothic,* was met with both warm and lukewarm reception. The vision of reconstructing the Gothic house, with a bronze sculpture of the couple in front remains only a vision. Mayor Don Canney approved of the concept by Gary Anderson of Munsell, Fultz & Zirbel Advertising Agency.

Personal Notes and Letters from Nan

A May, 1980 letter to John and Joan Zug from Nan:

"We were given a turkey for Christmas, and since we are having such cool days, and it might turn hot suddenly, I decided to bake the turkey and invited friends in to help eat it. What a mess. I baked it for four hours, and it wasn't done then, and it was only a ten-pound turkey. The recipe said it should be baked less than three hours. I'm a wreck now and feel like I'm never going to get rested again.

"Frank is 94, and he still thinks of me as a school girl, and that I should never get tired, and that a good night's sleep should put me back in the pink. Gosh! I can't think of anything worse than to live to be 94, like he is, and I suppose I will. It would be just like me to live to be 100. How I would hate it."

In a phone conversation, Nan said Frank wanted cherry pie daily.

An April 16, 1988, letter to Joan Liffring-Zug Bourret from Pauline (Cogswell) and Nan:

"Your letter arrived and I read it to Nan. …she is still in LeHavre Com. Hospital. She was doing fairly well until March 24th when she fell and broke her other hip. She was in Kaiser Redwood City Hospital until April 4th when she returned to LeHavre. She is plenty miserable. Lots of pain in the hip. …They get her up for therapy which wears her out, but mostly she is living in bed, even for meals.

"Park Rinard, her friend from Washington, D.C., was here from Tues. until this morning. They had a good visit but Nan is more lonely than ever today.

"Nan does not have a telephone in her room. …I asked her today if she wanted a telephone in her room. She said, 'absolutely not' with much emphasis.

"Nan appreciated the clipping you sent. Ed Green's wealth was surely a surprise. Nan has no clipping about Ed Green's funeral.

"Nan has not been able to write letters for some time and, of course, not now."

Best wishes, Pauline and Nan

My Friendship with Dear Nan

by Martha von Martinitz Rozen

Editor's note: *Martha's father was a pioneer medical doctor in Cedar Rapids, Iowa. Her sister Pauline and husband Rodney Cogswell were Nan's friends who supervised her care during her final years spent in a nursing home in northern California.*

My friendship with Nan goes back many years to Cedar Rapids, Iowa. We were neighbors. Our backyards were separated by an alley where horsedrawn wagons delivered groceries and milk. Nan and Grant attended schools with my older sisters and brothers.

At age six or seven, I wandered across the alley, for the first time, to see the goat tethered to the Wood's barn. We had a cat, chickens and pigeons but nothing compared to the goat! Nan rushed out of the kitchen to make sure I kept a safe distance from their nanny goat. Then she invited me in for cookies.

After that first meeting, I traipsed into their yard frequently, knowing I'd be welcome. Sometimes, Nan took me in to see valentines she was making. Or, it might be brightly colored May Day baskets of wallpaper, or Christmas decorations. Most often, she gave me a sample to take home. Nan was fun—and always making pretty things.

But she liked playing tricks, too. One summer day when I was admiring the nanny goat, she said, "Follow me, I'll show you a live plum." That puzzled me. High up in their plum tree, slightly hidden by leaves, was a small dark object. By a stretch of the imagination, it could be an overripe plum that somehow was slowly changing its outline. Nan convinced me it was a live plum. Days later, after everyone was told about the "live plum," she explained the mystery. It was a small, curled-up bat hanging by its feet. There were many bats in barns and trees in our area. We were scared out of our wits when they flew around and suddenly swooped down towards us.

Grant died when my family was living in Chicago. Father had retired from his medical practice and my brothers were established in business. Nan invited several family members to attend memorial services for Grant at the Chicago Art Institute. I was not invited and did not see her at that time.

Almost thirty years later, after Grant's death, I rediscovered Nan through a news item telling of her lawsuit against several television celebrities for defaming Grant's famous painting, *American Gothic*. The farmer's daughter (Nan) had been depicted "topless."

Nan was living in Riverside, California. Her husband, Ed Graham, died several years before. I resided in the Palm Springs area where my husband was a college teacher. It was a short drive to Riverside.

What a happy reunion! Nan was the same jovial person I remembered as a youngster when we left Iowa. She remarked, "It was as though the many years had not intervened since our good-bye in Cedar Rapids."

Soon, I realized how engrossed Nan was with keeping alive the esteemed memory of her brother Grant. She carefully analyzed everything written or spoken about him. She was quick to correct or criticize uncomplimentary remarks. Her devotion to him was uppermost in her mind.

Secondly, came her delight in entertaining. Other former Cedar Rapids friends located Nan through the same news item I had read. What beautiful, innovative house and garden parties she gave for the newly found old friends!

Nan lived in Riverside more years than in any other place, including Iowa. She was an honorary member of both the Riverside Art Museum and the Buena Park Wax Museum where the *American Gothic* figures were reproduced.

However, she kept close ties with Iowa friends and participated in the annual "Grant Wood Art Festival" in Anamosa, Iowa.

After my husband and I moved back to the San Francisco Bay area, Nan came often to our home for special occasions. She was a "surprise guest" at one of our parties. The other guests were art patrons who had been with us on a tour of art museums in France. Nan introduced herself as having the face that appeared in more places and on more objects than any one face in the U.S. She gave several more clues but not until she said, "The man beside me holds a pitchfork," did someone guess her identity. Everyone was astonished and couldn't believe that this pleasant, friendly person was the sour-faced, stern looking spinster in *American Gothic* painted by her brother.

The holidays of Christmas and the New Year were Nan's favorites. When she spent them with us, she enjoyed adding her touch to my decor.

Nan's eyesight gradually failed. She was young in spirit but living alone with poor vision was becoming unbearable. She sold her Riverside home and moved to northern California, a short distance from us. Many afternoons we reminisced together. She was far more

Nan Wood Graham, inspite of being blind and bedfast, enjoyed the contact with old friends including Park Rinard shown with her. Park was Grant's secretary during his Iowa City years. Nan had endured many eye operations, a broken hip and other problems but kept a spirit of cheerfulness. Prints of American Gothic *and of her mother, the model for* Woman With Plant(s), *hung by her bed. Her 90th birthday party was held bedside.*

Photo from John Fitzpatrick

knowledgeable than I regarding people, activities, and even my family during my young years in Cedar Rapids.

A high point and memorable occasion for everyone was Nan's 90th birthday celebration held in the convalescent residence where she spent her last years. Many friends flew in to wish her well and remained several days to chat and cheer her. The press photographed and interviewed her. She was on television. There were newspaper accounts with pictures of her in color. Cards and letters arrived. The week-long activities gave her quite a boost!

Nan's 91st birthday was celebrated with less fanfare, but her ardent admirers came to greet her. In December of this same year, 1990, Nan died. Her friends gathered in our home amidst Christmas surroundings and decorations—quite befitting and reminiscent of Nan's happy holidays with us in bygone years.

Last Will and Testament
Nan Wood Graham

Summary by Julie Jensen McDonald

"I asked why she was always pessimistic, expecting the worst? And her answer was 'because then I am never disappointed.'"

— Rodney Cogswell, husband of
Pauline von Martinitz Cogswell,
Executor of the Nan Wood Graham Estate

Nan Wood Graham's character is seen clearly in the brief will she wrote by hand despite failing eyesight in 1986. She directed that her bills be paid first, "These will be few and current, as I have always gone on a cash basis, and all bills have been paid immediately."

With $261,827.25 to dispense, she was much better off than she had been in her early life. Even in death, Grant Wood had taken care of his sister.

Although she had had a falling out with her husband's children, who became known to her only after Ed's death, she still refers to them as stepdaughters and stepson and leaves them what she considers to be fair: the insurance that was their father's only worldly possession at the time of his death to the girls, two cemetery lots to the son. One lot was occupied by his father's grave, and Nan suggested that he sell both and "use the proceeds to bring his father and mother together," and gave him additional money for those expenses.

The first version of the will makes a bequest to Calvary Presbyterian Church in Riverside, but she changes that a year later, giving the money to the Union Rescue Mission, Los Angeles, to aid destitute women and children. She knew all too well what destitution was like, remembering her mother's struggles to rear fatherless children with no money. She also left money to Riverside County Coalition for Alternatives to Domestic Violence.

Among the others she remembered were Pauline von Martinitz Cogswell and Rodney V. Cogswell. Pauline von Martinitz lived in Cedar Rapids during Nan's youth, and she and her husband, a former minister, devoted themselves to Nan's welfare in her last years.

Park Rinard, Grant's secretary, his wife and three of his children were remembered, as was Edwin Green, the Iowa City newspaper editor who was a close friend of both Grant and Nan.

She made a bequest to Ernie and Joanne Buresh of Anamosa "in payment for a business matter taken care of by Ernie at no charge to me." The Bureshes contributed the first part of their legacy to a fund for building the clock tower of the National Czech & Slovak Museum & Library in Cedar Rapids, Iowa.

Asking that her executor, Pauline Cogswell take her ashes to Anamosa Riverside Cemetery to be buried beside her mother and Grant, she wrote, "If my friends so desire, I would appreciate it if they gather together at their convenience, reminisce, drink a toast to me and say a prayer in my behalf. I would also appreciate a prayer at my grave. My headstone is already in place."

Her friends did so desire, meeting to remember Nan at the Grant Wood Tourism Center in Anamosa following her graveside ceremony. The date was February 13, 1991, forty-nine years and one day after Grant Wood's death. Grant and his little sister were together again.

Ernie Buresh, friend and confidant

"I became acquainted with Nan Wood Graham before the first Grant Wood Art Festival. A group of us from Anamosa, including the Don Penners and the Gerald Browns, were excited about Grant Wood being from here and decided to contact Nan to see if she would attend the first Grant Wood Festival. It was to be held in Anamosa and Stone City, the second weekend of June, for two days.

"There was a parade on Main Street, an antique show, a juried art show at the Stone City barn, and even a dance with Sammy Kaye and his orchestra. The Antioch (Grant Wood's) School was open.

"Nan brought a friend, Rita Campbell, a writer from San Diego, and a stepdaughter to stay with us also. Pauline and Rodney Cogswell, her close friends, came from California. It was a special time.

"The letters and visits at festival time continued for many years. Nan gave us an antique silver syrup pitcher that had been a wedding present from a relative of hers. Nan gave Mildred Brown many personal treasures. They are on display by appointment in the old Doctor's Office on Main Street in Anamosa.

"Nan stayed in our home for the last time before she left for New York to be on the 'Good Morning America' show. They talked to her by phone in our den before she left to view the Grant Wood Exhibit which would show *American Gothic* for the first time in many years outside of Chicago. KGAN-TV station came to our home to interview her. She was creative, entertaining, and full of fun, but she was already losing her sight. One of the stepdaughters accompanied her. The other daughter would be going with her to Minneapolis when the exhibit opened there.

"Most of our correspondence dealt with her finances. She'd write about her investments, asking questions, and periodically, whenever there was a change, she sent me an inventory of her assets.

"Her 90th birthday celebration at the LeHavre Convalescent Hospital in Menlo Park, California, was special. With her sight gone, she still was 'up' for the day and spoke very well. I visited with her the next day in her room. This was to be our last personal visit.

"It was a surprise to be included in her will."

Editor's note: The Bureshes contributed their legacy in memory of Nan to the National Czech & Slovak Museum & Library toward the cost of the Clock Tower.

Bank President Ernie Buresh of Anamosa, front right, sits by Nan Wood Graham surrounded by staff of the City National Bank, Cedar Rapids. Nan visited the bank when the book This Is Grant Wood Country *was released in 1978. Billboards with a parody of* American Gothic *are posted along the highways near Anamosa on either side of the town in Jones County where Grant Wood was born over a century ago. Downtown Anamosa, Iowa, has a Grant Wood Tourism Center with the parody collection of Price Slate on display. A section of a mural, created by Grant Wood and his students, salvaged from an old hotel in Council Bluffs is also on display.*

NAN WOOD GRAHAM

Memorial Gathering For
NAN WOOD GRAHAM

Riverside Cemetery
Anamosa, Iowa
February 13, 1991

Opening — *E. J. Buresh*
Placing of Wreath — *Mildred Brown*
Invitation for Comments
From Friends
Prayer — *Rev. Billy Duay,*
First Congregational Church

— You are invited to the Grant Wood
Tourism Center immediately
following the Ceremony —

The Anamosa cemetery where Grant Wood, Nan Wood Graham, brother John, and their parents are buried. The lion in the background is at the gravesite of their uncle, Clarence Wood.

Myths About Grant Wood

by John Zug

John Zug researched facts for eight years on behalf of Nan Wood Graham for her biography My Brother, Grant Wood.

After a prominent person dies, and after the entire peer group has passed on, new generations learn about that person from what has been written about him or her. In stories the difference between true and false may become elusive. Those who agreed or disagreed with, or liked or disliked that person, can be expected to write totally different versions. And then there are the myths.

Most of us don't have to worry about such matters, but consider George Washington. He died unaware that a concocted story by an itinerant pastor—something about a cherry tree—would create his image for generations of school children. "Myths After Lincoln" made an entire book.

How could an Iowa farm boy who became an artist get caught up in a battle of the myths? After all, Grant Wood was not a president. If we all kept quiet, wouldn't those myths die in time? Or if we all kept quiet would the myths and falsehoods live on while the truth withered on the vine? Who can tell? This is a story about myths and falsehoods that surrounded Grant Wood during his lifetime and later.

Nan Wood Graham knew which writer originated each of the Grant Wood myths and falsehoods. She wanted the record set straight, but she did not want their names used. She thought they all deserved obscurity. They all tended to read each other's work and reuse it. The newspaper art critics involved were in New York, Chicago, San Francisco, and elsewhere.

Various student writers at the University of Iowa were involved. These writers telegraphed their stories. One writer might serve papers in Chicago, Des Moines, Omaha, and possibly another one or two. This group of papers was known as his "string," and he was a "stringer." Another might send stories to papers in Cedar Rapids, Davenport, Minneapolis, and so on. There were more than two stringers in Iowa City. Each string was limited to papers that did not compete with each other. A stringer was paid by the column inch. When he graduated, he sold his string of papers to another student.

The greatest weakness of this system was that payment by the inch encouraged padding and rewarded the writer who could stir up a controversy, one that could be rehashed day after day. Eventually this system was destroyed, but it was in effect during Grant Wood's time in Iowa City.

Grant Wood would have known nothing about stringers, but he became so irritated with one that he refused to talk to him at all, even by telephone. Nan Wood Graham knew who it was.

When Grant Wood died, this young man was determined to write a biography of Grant Wood and to be first on the market. He had not been able to talk with Grant Wood, and now Nan Wood Graham would have nothing to do with him. So, apparently, he simply made up a good part of the book he wrote. He also picked up errors of other writers, and other writers picked up his tall tales. The authorized Grant Wood biography was to have been written by Grant Wood's secretary, Park Rinard. He was given much written material. It is now fifty years after Grant Wood's death, and that biography has never surfaced.

Early in 1976, Nan Wood Graham asked me to edit her story of her brother. In my spare time, I worked about five years on this project. The late Mrs. Graham, who then lived in Riverside, California, previously had been advised to seek help from a California writer who had authored six books. After a dinner with Mrs. Graham, this author took out pencil and paper and said: "Now tell me everything bad that you know about your brother." Nan was shocked. "Well," he said, "We've got to do something! We'll start by giving him red hair."

This is an example of the compulsive urge to fictionalize. "Docudrama" is one word for it, as though a label could legitimize dishonesty or contempt for the truth.

In Grant Wood's entire life, he never appeared on any stage as an actor (although once in high school he played the hind end of a horse), yet consider what was written about him:

"When they gave 'The Queen's Husband,' he took the part of the king's secretary and wore a peaked helmet during a disturbance at the palace. No helmet large enough for him could be found, and the one he wore sat on top of his head and teetered back and forth. On opening night he hurried onto the stage to announce: 'The fighting has started, your Majesty. The revolutionists broke through the first line of barricades on the esplanade, and tried to set fire to the city. ...' As he spoke these words, he jerked his head back, the helmet teetered too far and fell. Grant caught the helmet in his hands. He tried to save the situation by finishing his line, which was 'we caught it just in time!' This brought down the house, and it was several minutes before the production could proceed."

Elizabeth North Hoyt wrote in the *Cedar Rapids Gazette* of Sunday, December 3, 1944: "It seems a shame that Colonel James Yuill should be deprived of this, his only bid to Thespian fame. For it was Jim, not Grant, who played the king's secretary and brought down the house with his unpremeditated helmet-juggling. ..."

The same author who goofed on the above story wrote that "although his head was large, his eyes were small."

He also wrote: "To Grant, making jewelry and decorative items in the school's shop could hardly be considered work. He had been doing things like that for the fun of it. The fact was that he had no inclination for what was called regular work, and couldn't apply himself to it. ...Grant Wood hardly looked for work, though he sometimes came upon it."

For the truth, consult a 1935 article: "Wood was born on an Iowa farm, and from his tenth year has been self-supporting. He has been a gardener, farmhand, carpenter, builder, and night watchman in a morgue in Minneapolis. At one time he was a jeweler's assistant; at another in Chicago, he owned a shop in which he designed, executed, and sold metal ornaments of all kinds. He has been a country schoolmaster, a teacher of art in high schools, and at present is teaching art at the University of Iowa. ..."

Even that author missed a few occupations, principally interior decorating. Grant Wood started an interior decorating business before World War I and carried it on until the Stone City era of 1932–33. David Turner often found clients, and eventually hired Wood to decorate the Turner Mortuary.

In 1935 a Chicago newspaper article stated: "Wood is a sturdy, four-square son of the Middle West, an odd mixture of small town shrewdness and exemplary manners." In 1937, in a national magazine, the same author stated: "He is the soul of tact, and with a disarming amiability that makes aggressiveness unnecessary, a man who can rise to a state of ecstasy without getting excited. But at bottom he is a shrewd fellow, one with whom it would be unwise to trade horses or attempt to outwit in his own sphere. ...He is neither greedy nor greatly productive. ...Accustomed to economies and frugal in his desires, he lives well within be his income, which ranges from five to ten thousand dollars a year."

These statements were way off the mark, and they were widely reprinted. Asked about it, Mrs. Graham wrote to me: "The article that called Grant 'shrewd' was written while Grant was living. He did not take offense at it. In fact, I think he was rather amused. ..."

Her reaction was most unusual, because the comments were false. Grant Wood was naive, not shrewd. He literally gave away all the keys to his own house, then couldn't get in. Did he live within his income? False again. Grant Wood paid little attention to money. He carried currency loose in his pocket, and never failed to be surprised when someone handed him back a dollar or more that floated to the floor when he reached for his handkerchief. He wrote checks as long as he had a blank one to write on, and always was surprised when his account was overdrawn. He was not disrespectful of money. He simply had a disregard for it. As a result, he did not live within his income, and it is an error to say that he did.

Many critics made the error of classifying Grant Wood as a satirist. Grant Wood said: "Of course I have been satirical, but I have to keep insisting that I am not a satirist so that people won't get an easy and incorrect notion of what I am about. It is always easier to judge an artist by a label than by what he does, and often such judgment is irritating to an artist."

Wood conceded that *Daughters of Revolution* was satire. He said there was some satire in *American Gothic,* although he did not consider it to be primarily satire. Repeatedly, after *American Gothic* in 1930, critics found satire where there was none. After *Portrait of Nan* was viciously attacked by a New York critic who assumed it was satire, Wood never exhibited it again, but hung it over his own fireplace. In 1936 *Spring Turning* got a bad press. One critic said Wood was "making fun of nature."

A New York newspaperman wrote in 1935 that in World War I Grant Wood nearly died of anthrax at Camp Dodge, north of Des Moines. He said Wood had been reported dead but was found—thin and with a long beard. As a result of this error, a 1937 article in a national magazine stated: "At Camp Dodge an attack of anthrax nearly finished him." Six years later it was repeated in a book: "At Camp Dodge...he contracted anthrax and nearly died." Two pages later: "He had a thyroid condition for which he had been given medical treatment in the Army." Someone wrote that he had pyorrhea.

Nan Wood Graham, who received almost daily letters from her brother during World War I, says the true version is that influenza was of epidemic proportions at Camp Dodge, as it was throughout the nation, with many deaths. Wood became ill and was presumed to have influenza. He became part of a truckload of ill soldiers taken to the hospital, but he did not have flu and was released. What he had was an attack of appendicitis. The offending appendix was taken out three years later.

One author wrote: "Grant said he got the idea for those trees from the bulbous trees on his mother's Haviland china." In 1951 this error was repeated in the sound track of a movie on the lives of six artists, five of them old masters dating from the 15th century, and Grant Wood, representing the 20th century. The error was repeated in local newspapers in 1953 in an article reporting on the movie. Mrs. Graham said: "Grant could not have said that. Our china was the Moss-Rose pattern. Our everyday china had a gold band and three-leaf clover in the center."

A 1937 article stated that Grant Wood "is remembered by the old-timers in Cedar Rapids as the boy who minded the doctor's horse." Six years later this error was repeated in a book which stated: "Grant for some time looked after the horse of Dr. Richard Lord up the street." The truth is that Grant Wood milked Dr. Lord's cow each morning and evening. Wood also took care of one horse, but that animal belonged to another neighbor named Woitishek.

When viewed according to their tendency to reverse the man's true personality or character, other errors and myths dwindle off in relative significance, but not in total numbers.

• Error: Dr. McKeeby's posing for *American Gothic* "didn't require many trips to the studio." Fact: There were no trips at all; the artist went to Dr. McKeeby's office, and he posed there.

• Error: Nan's apron, "which Grant picked out of a mail-order catalog and had sent from Chicago…" Mrs. Graham said: "I made the apron."

• Error: "Grant helped coach one community drama group to a state championship won at the University of Iowa in 1932." Mrs. Graham said: "Grant never helped coach anybody in drama. Art was his bag."

• Error: "Thinking a rubber cigarette was a worm, a chicken gobbled it and died a slow death of strangulation when the cigarette stuck in the poor fowl's gullet." Mrs. Graham said the chick, which she holds in *Portrait of Nan,* gobbled the rubber cigarette all right, and from then on chased down all loose cigarette stubs. But it lived through it all, was given to David Turner's janitor, proved to be a good layer and a good mother, and had a long and productive life.

• Error: Several accounts have given the artist red hair and others pink hair. Mrs. Graham said: "This myth started when Grant came home from Paris with a sandy beard that he called pink." She said his hair was dishwater blond even though the beard he once grew turned out sandy.

• Error: David Turner was kicked by a mule, and retaliated by sending it uninvited to Grant Wood at the Stone City Colony and Art School. Mrs. Graham says Turner gave the mule to the postmaster, and her brother was in no way involved.

• Error: "He had gone a few times to the Peoples' Unitarian Church, almost his only church-going, and he continued to take part in the activities of a liberal group that formed there." Mrs. Graham said he was asked to talk there on two occasions and did so, and those were the only two times he was there.

• Error: David Turner "had 44 Grant Wood paintings, and 14 of Nan's." Nan said: "I never painted 14 in my life. David owned two."

• Error: When Grant Wood was two years old his cousin Clairbel Weaver predicted that he would become an artist. Mrs. Graham said: "Clairbel told me this is false. She said the first she ever heard such a story was when she saw it in print."

• Error: "Next to his mother, the person he knew best was his sister Nan. Ever since he had begun to walk, he had been determined that she should be an artist." Mrs. Graham said it is preposterous to suppose that Grant Wood, at age eleven, was determined that his two-year-old sister must become an artist. "Nothing was ever said to me about being an artist. I wanted to be a dress designer and made a lot of kooky, far-out dresses. Grant encouraged me to do and to be whatever I wanted to."

• Error: The Weavers homesteaded next to the Woods. Fact: The Weavers were not farmers in New York state or in Iowa, and never homesteaded. The grandfather of Nan and Grant was an innkeeper, later sheriff of Jones County, and still later a Cedar Rapids automobile dealer. On the death of her husband, Hattie Weaver Wood moved to Cedar Rapids to be near her parents; that is why Grant Wood was a Cedar Rapidian.

• Error: Their father didn't read the Bible much, and didn't pray, even before meals. Mrs. Graham said: "For years, Father was superintendent of Mother's Sunday School. It was there that he and Mother met. He was devout, and prayed before each meal."

- Error: Grant Wood was a sissy, bringing one teacher two watercolors. Fact: They were required art work.
- Error: Grant got into fights at school, seldom forgot an offense, and was defiant when beaten. Mrs. Graham said this is as untrue as the sissy story, and the opposite of her brother's real personality.
- Error: "Grant was the kind who took offense, suffered over trivialities, and became mired in controversies." Mrs. Graham said hundreds knew her brother's personality to be the reverse—never petty, never concerned over trivialities.
- Error: Grant never did farmwork. Mrs. Graham said: "By the age of ten, when we had to leave the farm, he had done every farm job within his strength. In his teens, he spent an entire summer as a farmhand, and later spent summers helping Uncle Clarence on the Wood farm near Anamosa."
- Error: His high school art teacher held his watercolor under a faucet to blur the lines. Mrs. Graham said this is a fabrication.
- Error: He retouched the work of his own students until they were unable to recognize it. Fact: He did not touch or retouch the work of students.
- Error: At his Cedar Rapids high school, there was no art in the curriculum. Mrs. Graham said: "Art was offered in all the schools, and it was his main study in high school."
- Error: He had "sponsors" and "chief sponsors." Mrs. Graham said: "If anyone was Grant's sponsor, it was David Turner. They were neighbors and friends from the time Grant arrived in Cedar Rapids. But my brother had been employed full time in the Cedar Rapids schools for several years before the start of the relationship that led to the use of the term 'sponsor.' David Turner was a sponsor, although both he and Grant in those days considered themselves merely as friends. Grant had many friends, and some of them were very helpful."
- Error: He was often seen on the streets of Cedar Rapids, peering into the faces of strangers. Mrs. Graham said: "As untrue as a statement by the same writer that he couldn't look strangers in the eye."
- Error: He bought his first car in 1922, a dismal, secondhand affair that caused people to ask him when he expected delivery of the rest of the car. Fact: He paid $900 for an almost new Overland which had been driven but little.

• Error: In Paris he went to the Quat-z-Arts Ball dressed as a fish, was admitted, and escorted down a long hall and through a door back onto the street. Fact: He went to the Paris ball, was welcomed, and stayed. The account of it is in his scrapbook. It was to the BeauxArts Ball in Cedar Rapids that he went dressed as a fish. Dr. Florence Johnson and Miss Frances Prescott had him in the net. They won first prize.

• Error: From Paris he brought home a beret and several dozen gray Canton flannel shirts. Mrs. Graham says such shirts were beyond his means; he never owned one, and never owned a beret.

• Error: "His painting took a sensational turn for the first time after he moved to #5 Turner Alley. …Combining some of the worst features of surrealists and neo-meditationists, he painted a piece of music with tangents going this way and that. …The painting was not well-received." Mrs. Graham said: "Ed and I had a phonograph. Grant liked 'Song of India.' For a joke, he made a painting of it. He liked to hang it upside down with a $1,000 price tag on it. It was a joke, and this was long before he lived at #5 Turner Alley."

• Error: He kept a forge outside #5 Turner Alley. Fact: No forge.

• Error: He had painted with barn paint, egg whites, and strained honey. Mrs. Graham said: "He never used any of these in his life. I've heard that Benton used eggs."

• Error: He once said, "The model is only the bones. I really paint what I see in my head." Mrs. Graham said: "He detested that type of painting."

• Error: Because he did not like *Woman With Plant(s),* he photographed his mother and persuaded Cousin Clairbel Weaver to substitute the photo for a print of the painting. He kept the photo on his own mantel. Mrs. Graham said: "No photo, no truth to story. If he had not liked the painting, Grant would have continued to work on it. He considered *Woman With Plant(s)* one of his best works."

• Error: "Whenever one of Turner's funeral clients asked him to dispose of leftover flowers, the best were brought to the studio and Grant painted them. Flower pictures always sold well." Mrs. Graham said: "Grant painted only four flower pictures, as I recall. One was of sunflowers, another was of calendulas. None were of funeral flowers. The story is false."

Hattie Weaver Wood

The most famous myth associated with Grant Wood is still alive, but appears less and less. When *American Gothic* was unveiled, the man and woman in the painting were described as "the farmer and his wife." In a denial that was long unsuccessful, Grant Wood protested that they were a small-town man and his daughter. His models were his dentist and his sister Nan.

Of the myths and errors, the ones most to be regretted are those that are simply made up—"docudrama." The fact is that the true story would have been of more interest, and of more lasting interest, than the falsehoods and fictions. Fortunately, by a man's works shall he be known, and Grant Wood's paintings and lithographs live on.